Canto is an imprint offering a range of titles, classic and more recent, across a broad spectrum of subject areas and interests. History, literature, biography, archaeology, politics, religion, psychology, philosophy and science are all represented in Canto's specially selected list of titles, which now offers some of the best and most accessible of Cambridge publishing to a wider readership.

P9-BZK-861

Beethoven. Miniature portrait on ivory
by Christian Hornemann, 1803

MEMORIES OF BEETHOVEN

GERHARD VON BREUNING

Memories of
Beethoven

From the House of the
Black-Robed Spaniards

EDITED BY
MAYNARD SOLOMON

Translated from the German
by Henry Mins and Maynard Solomon

CAMBRIDGE
UNIVERSITY PRESS

Published by the Press Syndicate of the University of Cambridge
The Pitt Building, Trumpington Street, Cambridge CB2 1RP
40 West 20th Street, New York, NY 10011–4211, USA
10 Stamford Road, Oakleigh, Melbourne 3166, Australia

© Cambridge University Press 1992

First published 1992
Canto edition 1995

Printed in Great Britain at the University Press, Cambridge

A catalogue record for this book is available from the British Library

Library of Congress cataloguing in publication data
Breuning, Gerhard von. b. 1813.
[Aus dem Schwarzspanierhause. English]
Memories of Beethoven: from the house of the black-robed Spaniards /
Gerhard von Breuning: edited by Maynard Solomon; translated from the
German by Henry Mins and Maynard Solomon.
p. cm.
Translation of: Aus dem Schwarzspanierhause.
Includes bibliographical references and index.
ISBN 0 521 48489 8
1. Beethoven, Ludwig van, 1770–1827.
2. Composers – Austria – Biography.
I. Title.
ML410.B4B813 1992
780'.92–dc20
[B] 91–44025 CIP MN

ISBN 0 521 48489 8 paperback

CONTENTS

ILLUSTRATIONS

ABBREVIATIONS

AMZ	*Allgemeine musikalische Zeitung*
Anderson	Emily Anderson, ed., *The Letters of Beethoven*, 3 vols. (London, 1961).
BJ	*Beethoven-Jahrbuch.* 1st ser. (1908–1909), ed. Theodor von Frimmel; 2nd ser. (1953–), vols. 1–8, ed. Paul Mies and Joseph Schmidt-Görg, vol. 9, ed. Hans Schmidt and Martin Staehelin, vol. 10, ed. Martin Staehelin
Breuning	Gerhard von Breuning, *Aus dem Schwarzspanierhause* (Vienna, 1874)
Conversation Books	See Köhler–Herre–Beck
DSB	Deutsche Staatsbibliothek, Berlin
Frimmel, *Handbuch*	Theodor von Frimmel, *Beethoven-Handbuch*, 2 vols. (Leipzig, 1926)
GdMF	Gesellschaft der Musikfreunde, Vienna
Kalischer	Breuning, *Aus dem Schwarzspanierhause*, 2nd edn., ed. Alfred C. Kalischer (Berlin and Leipzig, 1907)
Kerst	Friedrich Kerst, ed., *Die Erinnerungen an Beethoven*, 2 vols. (Stuttgart, 1913)
Kinsky–Halm	Georg Kinsky, *Das Werke Beethovens. Thematisch-bibliographisches Verzeichnis seiner sämtlichen vollendeten Kompositionen*, completed and ed. Hans Halm (Munich, 1955)
Köhler–Herre–Beck	Karl-Heinz Köhler, Grita Herre, and Dagmar Beck, ed., *Ludwig van Beethovens Konversationshefte*, vols. 1–9 (Leipzig, 1968–1988)
Ley, *Beethoven als Freund*	Stephan Ley, ed., *Beethoven als Freund der Familie Wegeler-v. Breuning* (Bonn, 1927)

MGG	*Die Musik in Geschichte und Gegenwart*, ed. Friedrich Blume et al.
Moscheles	[Charlotte Moscheles], *The Life of Moscheles by his Wife*, translated by A. D. Coleridge, 2 vols. (London, 1873)
NBJ	*Neues Beethoven Jahrbuch*, ed. Adolf Sandberger
Nottebohm, *Beethoveniana*	Gustav Nottebohm, *Beethoveniana* (Leipzig and Winterthur, 1872)
Schindler	Anton Schindler, *Biographie von Ludwig van Beethoven*, 3rd edn., 2 vols (Münster, 1860)
Schindler–MacArdle	Anton Schindler, *Beethoven As I Knew Him*, ed. Donald W. MacArdle (London and Chapel Hill, 1966), translation of Schindler
Schindler–Moscheles	Anton Schindler, *The Life of Beethoven*, ed. Ignaz Moscheles (Boston, 1841), translation of 1st edn. of Schindler, *Biographie von Ludwig van Beethoven* (Münster, 1840)
Smolle, *Wohnstätten*	Kurt Smolle, *Wohnstätten Ludwig van Beethovens von 1792 bis zu seinem Tod* (Bonn and Munich-Duisberg, 1970)
Solomon, *Beethoven*	Maynard Solomon, *Beethoven* (New York, 1977)
Solomon, *Beethoven Essays*	Maynard Solomon, *Beethoven Essays* (Cambridge, Mass., 1988)
Sonneck	O. G. Sonneck, *Beethoven: Impressions of Contemporaries* (New York, 1926)
Tagebuch	"Beethoven's Tagebuch of 1812–1818," in Solomon, *Beethoven Essays*
Thayer	Alexander Wheelock Thayer, *Ludwig van Beethovens Leben*, 3 vols. (Berlin, 1866, 1872, 1879)
Thayer–Deiters	A. W. Thayer, *Ludwig van Beethovens Leben*, vol. 1, 2nd edn., ed. Hermann Deiters (Leipzig, 1901)
Thayer–Deiters–Riemann	A. W. Thayer, *Ludwig van Beethovens Leben*, ed. and enlarged by Hermann Deiters and Hugo Riemann, 5 vols. (Leipzig, 1907–1917; reissued 1922–1923)

Thayer–Forbes	*Thayer's Life of Beethoven*, ed. Elliot Forbes, 2 vols. (Princeton, 1964; rev. 1967)
Thayer–Krehbiel	A. W. Thayer, *The Life of Ludwig van Beethoven*, ed. and completed by Henry E. Krehbiel, 3 vols. (New York, 1921)
Wegeler–Ries	Franz Wegeler and Ferdinand Ries, *Biographische Notizen über Ludwig van Beethoven* (Coblenz, 1838). *Nachtrag* (Supplement) by Wegeler (Coblenz, 1845)
Wegeler–Ries Eng. edn.	*Beethoven Remembered: The Biographical Notes of Franz Wegeler and Ferdinand Ries*, translated by Frederick Noonan (Arlington, 1987)
WoO	Werk(e) ohne Opuszahl (work[s] without opus number) in the listing of Kinsky-Halm

EDITOR'S INTRODUCTION

Gerhard von Breuning's *Memories of Beethoven: From the House of the Black-Robed Spaniards* is a minor classic of the Beethoven literature, an important source for our knowledge of the composer's last years, and it has had an influence on biographies of the composer disproportionate to its modest size. As one of only three book-length essays on Beethoven's life written by people who knew him – the others being the *Biographische Notizen über Ludwig van Beethoven* by Franz Gerhard Wegeler and Ferdinand Ries, and the *Biographie von Ludwig van Beethoven* in several editions by Anton Schindler – it is cited frequently and confidently, so that Breuning's observations have become part of the warp and woof of all biographies of Beethoven, beginning with the standard nineteenth-century works by Alexander Wheelock Thayer, Ludwig Nohl, George Grove, among many others. First published in 1874, Breuning's book has been reprinted several times, and it has been substantially excerpted in various collections of Beethoven-memoirs by his contemporaries.[1] The text of the first edition was reprinted in Stephan Ley's *Beethoven als Freund der Familie Wegeler-v. Breuning* in 1927 and in a book illustrated by Wilhelm Thöny which appeared in 1954.[2] A second edition, containing a few additions and sketchy annotations by the prolific Beethoven scholar A. C. Kalischer, was published in 1907 and reprinted in 1970.[3] Despite its influence, Breuning's book has never been adequately annotated and never previously translated from the German into any language.

Gerhard von Breuning was born on August 28, 1813 in Vienna into a family whose close connections with Beethoven began in the 1780s in Bonn, and which, in the composer's later adolescence and young manhood, had been for him an ideal family at the time of his own family's rapid disintegration through conflict, sickness, and death. Together, Beethoven and the von Breunings moved in the cultured and enlightened circles in Bonn, warmly sharing cultural ideals and aspirations for social transformation, as their letters and entries in souvenir albums make clear.[4] Several years after Beethoven left Bonn to pursue his career in Vienna, Breuning's father Stephan also moved to the capital and lived out his life there as an employee of the

War Ministry. Stephan's relationship with Beethoven was both intimate and volatile, as close connections with the composer were likely to be, and their lives converged and diverged several times, with separations sometimes lasting months, even many years. However, their attachment was such that serious ruptures – including several of long duration – invariably ended in warm reconciliations. The last of these reconciliations took place in the summer of 1825, after a separation of more than a decade. Soon afterwards, Beethoven moved into the Schwarzspanierhaus, around the corner from the Breuning lodging in the Rothes Haus. From then until Beethoven's death on March 26, 1827, he was a frequent and welcome companion, if sometimes an uncouth and irascible one, of the Breuning family – Stephan, his second wife Constanze, and their three children, among whom was a daughter Marie and Gerhard, who was then twelve years old.

Gerhard was a keen observer of small details: of Beethoven's behavior at the table, on the street, and at work; of his physical appearance, his deafness (which the boy tested by pounding on the piano when the composer's head was turned), the curve of his fingers at the keyboard. He provides a minute description of the Schwarzspanierhaus exterior and the floor-plan of Beethoven's apartment within it; he reconstructs the placement of the furniture and the functional layout of the rooms. He tells us who Beethoven's visitors were; he describes his suspiciousness, withdrawal, and "fondness for sarcasm"; he reports Beethoven's repeated laments that he had never married; he remembers how the composer would sometimes solicit his nephew's opinion on a projected work; he recalls how Beethoven awaited the visits of Dr. Malfatti "as eagerly as those of a Messiah"; he even gives us material relevant to an understanding of Beethoven's creativity, for example, how he was reconciled to occasional periods of low productivity because he knew that his creativity was always restored "sooner or later." Breuning was gratified that Beethoven took such a strong liking to him, recalling with delight that Beethoven dubbed him with the affectionate pet-names "Ariel" and "Hosenknopf" (trouser-button), and that Beethoven took an interest in his musical studies, suggesting that he use Clementi's piano method and actually obtaining a copy of it for him. So complete is his sense of a merger between Beethoven and his own family that he recounts with evident pride, and without any sense of impropriety, the family tradition that Beethoven had been attracted to, or had even courted, both of Stephan von Breuning's wives. Gerhard is powerfully affected, not only by Beethoven's fame, but his personality: he wants to be a "good son" to Beethoven, in contrast to the "ungrateful" nephew Karl; he heard Beethoven's obsessive complaints about his nephew; he remembers the young man's suicide attempt in July 1826, the frantic ensuing strategy discussions, and his father's assumption of the nephew's guardianship in September; he interviewed the physician who was on duty when Beethoven visited his nephew in the City Hospital, and he describes Beethoven's departure for his brother's estate in Gneixendorf in late September 1826, where it was hoped that he would find relief from these crushing events. However, Beethoven was already mortally ill when he left Vienna, and he returned there in early December to lie in a sick-bed for three and a half months until his death.

It is as a clear-eyed witness of Beethoven's final illness and death-throes that Gerhard von Breuning shows himself at his most attractive. He probably did not visit the sick-bed as frequently as he later claimed or as frequently as Beethoven desired. In February 1827, for example, Stephan wrote in a conversation book: "Gerhard can hardly wait to visit you again; he hopes to do so in a few days."[5] In the event, he was there very often, sometimes for many days in a row, delivering food prepared by his mother, bearing messages between the two households, remaining to talk to Beethoven for a while. He was a welcome guest, entertaining, bright, and encouraging. He was always considerate, trying to steer the conversations in hopeful directions. On New Year's Eve, he writes, "Father, mother and I all wish you a happy new year and that the sickness will remain in the old year and that the new year will only bring you health."[6] He assures Beethoven that he is looking better; he talks about vacation trips that his father and Beethoven might take next summer; he chatters disconnectedly about a variety of subjects – the theater, concerts, personalities, and domestic issues. A bright boy, he knows a lot about many things – soldiers' pay, the price of an oil cloth to cover Beethoven's sheets, even about the taste of a Heuriger wine – and does not hesitate to voice his opinions. Mainly, however, the subject is Beethoven's health, comfort, and the progress of his medical treatment. In a characteristic conversation of January 1827, Gerhard writes:

How are you? – I'm not coughing, only if I run up the stairs. – Has your stomach become smaller? – You should sweat more, continuously. – ... Today you already ought to eat meat. – Have you taken an enema? You ought to take more of them. – Have you already read Walter Scott yet? – Would you perhaps like to read Schiller? – Would you like Schröck's World History? – Perhaps you'd like Sommer's travel descriptions. – I'll show it to you tomorrow. –[7]

Beethoven's responses can only be surmised, but there was obviously a ready and comfortable interchange between him and the boy. Subsequent entries similarly show Gerhard's rapid juxtaposition of conversational topics:

My teacher goes to the *Concerts spirituels* also. – This evening we're going to the Leopoldstadt Theater; I'm not sure whether father will go too. – I heard today that the bedbugs are tormenting and disturbing you so much that you are constantly being awakened from your sleep; but since you now need to sleep well, I'll bring you something to drive away the bedbugs ... – The doctor says that you need to eat meat. – How did the marrow dumplings taste? Marrow dumplings in the soup. – I have to leave, for I have something to do, because I'm going to the theater at 7.30. –[8]

Small descriptive touches bring several of Beethoven's friends and visitors to life:

Wolfmayer is so fond of you that when he sent his regards, tears came to his eyes, and he said, "The great man. Ach! Ach!" – He asked if you still have wine – Schindler says he doesn't like ham dumplings. – Don't be angry about it; let's talk about something else instead! ... – Malfatti is your best doctor. He cares for you very much. –[9]

But Gerhard doesn't conceal his feelings; once he says to Beethoven plainly, "Today you look very weary."[10] He has strong dislikes as well, and can be straightforward in expressing them, apparently without encouragement:

Holz cannot stand it if anyone he knows calls him false. – He is a great hypocrite ... – You are the best one of them all, the others are all scoundrels (*Lumpen*). – If you weren't so good-natured, you could ask him [Schindler?] also to pay for his board. – He likes your wine best.[11]

All of this gives us sufficient reason to trust Breuning as an authentic witness. And, indeed, although Breuning in his memoirs does not quote from his own entries in the conversation books,[12] the general tenor of his recollections is often confirmed by the surviving conversations. However, Breuning's book does not consist only of personal recollections. In addition to these he attempted to offer a more global overview of several important biographical areas: first, an outline history of the von Breuning family and its connection with Beethoven, beginning in the 1780s in Bonn; second, an account of Beethoven's relationship with Gerhard's father, Stephan von Breuning; third, a sampling of the anecdotal and descriptive literature on Beethoven; fourth, a chronology of and commentary on Beethoven's last year. In these, and in other passing observations, he relied not only upon family lore and his own recollections, but primarily upon the Beethoven literature existing at that time. On the credit side, this included Wegeler and Ries's honest and unpretentious little book,[13] from which Breuning took a good deal of his data about the Breuning family and its Beethoven connection; Gustav Nottebohm's irreproachable *Beethoveniana* (Leipzig and Winterthur, 1872); and the earlier volumes of the monumental and authoritative biographies of Beethoven by Thayer and Nohl, both of which were then in progress. Unfortunately, it also included the various editions, the last of which was published in 1860, of Schindler's famous biography of Beethoven, a book which has tainted all subsequent biographical studies because of its author's wide-ranging errors, prejudiced readings, deliberate misrepresentations, and forgeries.

In a complex web of fabrications, Schindler pretended to have been Beethoven's acquaintance from as early as 1814 and his close friend and associate from 1818 onward, with an interruption after spring 1824. Actually, however, Schindler's connection with Beethoven was almost wholly limited to the year and a half from late 1822 or early 1823 to spring 1824 and the three months from late December 1826 until March 1827.[14] He invented dozens of scenes, some of which have become legendary. He forged more than 150 passages in the conversation books. He appropriated large quantities of Beethoven's autograph scores, manuscript letters, conversation books, memorabilia, and key items from Beethoven's library. He invented deathbed conversations in which Beethoven authorized him to approach editor J. F. Rochlitz – now known to have been himself a notable forger of biographical accounts and documents[15] – to write his biography; he claimed implicit and verbal authorization for his own biographical efforts, although Beethoven had given such an authorization in writing to his trusted friend Karl Holz. He was concerned to make money from his stolen property: he offered some of Beethoven's scores to the publisher Schott's Sons as early as 1828 and to Breitkopf & Härtel at later dates.[16] Eventually, he sold a large part of the collection to the Royal Library in Berlin for 2000 thalers and a substantial lifetime annuity. He posed as an expert on the performance and meaning of Beethoven's music; indeed, many of the forged conversation book entries are intended not only to exaggerate the extent and depth of his relationship with Beethoven but to bolster his claims to authority in matters of performance practise and interpretation.

Neither Thayer's nor Nohl's biographies, though their publications commenced in the 1860s, had yet reached Beethoven's final decade when Breuning published his own book, nor had Thayer yet published his *Ein kritischer*

Beitrag zur Beethoven-Literatur (*A Critical Contribution to the Beethoven Literature*) (1877), which seriously began the deconstruction of Schindler's work, a process which culminated a century later in the demonstration by Grita Herre and Dagmar Beck of Schindler's forgeries in the conversation books.[17] Even before that startling exposure, Joseph Kerman had realistically summed up the problem of using Schindler's biography: "In short, every statement of fact and every shade of implication requires verification or, if verification is not possible, the stern exercise of judgment".[18] After Beck and Herre, prudence now suggests that where verification is not possible, none of Schindler's anecdotes, accounts, observations, or judgments may be relied upon.

At the time when Breuning was conducting his research and preparing his book for publication, Schindler's authority was at its very peak. Thus, it was inevitable that Breuning would draw upon Schindler for details of events that he had not himself witnessed. Indeed, he quotes or refers to a wide variety of data and anecdotes from Schindler, both from publications by Schindler and from his own conversations with him during a four-day visit to his home near Frankfurt in July 1863.[19] These materials (which are identified either by Breuning himself or in the editorial annotations) consist mostly of "characteristic anecdotes" about Beethoven, some of which may be true, some of which do not originate with Schindler in any event, and none of which significantly undermine the integrity of Breuning's effort. More seriously, however, Breuning also took over some of Schindler's prejudices and polemical attitudes. This is troublesome, because Schindler used his biography to vent his hostilities, to settle scores with his numerous enemies, both real and imaginary, and to attack those whom he despised, such as Beethoven's nephew Karl, his brother Johann, his sisters-in-law Johanna and Therese, along with Ignaz Moscheles, Holz, and the attending doctors.

Breuning unhesitatingly repeats several of Schindler's most spiteful fabrications – that Beethoven was mistreated by his brother at Gneixendorf; that his illness was caused by Johann's refusal to provide a closed carriage to Vienna during inclement weather; that nephew Karl, busy playing billiards, delayed several days before sending for a doctor, who turned out to be the thoroughly incompetent Dr. Andreas Wawruch; that the latter's botched medical treatment, together with the inhumane and mercenary attitudes of his former doctors, led to Beethoven's death. Breuning endorses Schindler's vengeful attacks on Dr. Wawruch, who, Schindler writes, "ruined him with too much medicine," and on Dr. Malfatti, who was unwilling to differ with a colleague, allegedly saying, "Tell Beethoven that as a master of harmony he will understand that I too have to live in harmony with my colleagues," a remark that supposedly brought Beethoven to tears.[20] But the conversation books show Wawruch to have been a conscientious and caring physician, who visited his patient at least once daily, who consulted with three other leading doctors about the diagnosis and course of treatment, and who tried to keep hope alive until the very end. That Schindler manufactured these charges after the fact is suggested by his letter to Moscheles of February 22, 1827, in which he cited the treatment by Wawruch and Malfatti without caveat, indicating that he was then in full accord with their course of treatment and knew that Beethoven's death was inevitable: "Judging by the present symptoms, dropsy will turn to consumption, for he is now worn to a skeleton, and yet his constitution will enable him to struggle for a long time against this painful death."[21] It was clear to the doctors from the start that Beethoven's condition was hopeless, that all that remained was to relieve his suffering – by diet, medication, topical treatment, and especially by tapping the huge amounts of accumulated fluid in his abdominal cavity. After the fourth and final tapping, Beethoven himself understood that he would not survive, saying: "My day's work is done; if a doctor could still be of use in my case, 'his name shall be called wonderful.'"[22]

Breuning's contribution to the belittling of Beethoven's relatives, friends, and doctors is troubling. So, though we naturally want to have his frank recollections of people and events, we also want to know where his opinions are not those of an eyewitness but are simply unfounded repetitions or elaborations of slanted accounts by others, as with his remarks about Beethoven's stay at his brother's estate in Gneixendorf in the fall of 1826 or his comments about Beethoven's sisters-in-law. Inasmuch as Breuning told Thayer that he had never personally seen either Johanna or Therese van Beethoven,[23] he clearly had no standing to write – and we have no need to credit – such statements as: "Karl was constantly under the evil influence of his mother, a dissipated woman, vulgar in feeling and vulgar in action." It was for reasons such as this that Frimmel remarked on Breuning's "marked prejudice" against Beethoven's brother, and Max Vancsa, a pioneer student of Beethoven's nephew, wrote that Breuning's book "is written with visible maliciousness and, despite its foundation in the author's youthful memoirs, contains many exaggerations and errors."[24] When Thayer wrote his *Kritischer Beitrag* in defense of Beethoven's brother against Schindler, he did not spare (though he did not name) Breuning. Concerning the latter's description of Johann cutting a ludicrous figure as he rode his phaeton through the Prater, Thayer remarked, "Johann has even become endlessly mocked on account of his horse and carriage," and he scathingly asked whether any virtuous purpose would have been served if Johann's horse had remained in Gneixendorf over the winter while its master was a pedestrian in Vienna.[25]

Unlike Schindler, however, Breuning did not willfully distort the historical record or seek to inflate his personal role in Beethoven's biography, apart from an occasional false note, as when he describes supposed conversations with Beethoven about projected works, the neglect of his music, and his thoughts on posterity. And despite Schindler's authority, Breuning maintained an independent position on some issues. For example we know from the conversation books that young Gerhard did not like Holz, but as a memoirist Breuning did not join Schindler in expunging Holz from the list of those in attendance on Beethoven at the close.[26] Similarly, despite Breuning's dislike of Johann van Beethoven, he does not deny, as Schindler does, Johann's constant attendance at the sickbed.[27]

Thus, like all memoirs and autobiographical accounts, Breuning's book requires a critical reading, a testing of its sources, and an awareness of possible distortions arising from failures of memory or from agendas of self-interest. It is only natural that we should wonder if Breuning – and Wegeler before him – might have exaggerated the role of the Breuning–Wegeler family in Beethoven's life; but the documents – contemporary letters, conversation books, entries in souvenir albums, reports of Beethoven's statements to third persons – reinforce their accounts. In Beethoven's letter to Wegeler of December 7, 1826, written upon the onset of his fatal illness, he remembered "all the love which you have always shown me, for instance, how you had my room whitewashed and thus gave me such a pleasant surprise, – and likewise all the kindnesses I have received from the Breuning family."[28] Stephan von Breuning was indeed one of Beethoven's closest friends from adolescence until death; his appointment as nephew Karl's guardian in September 1826 and later as executor of Beethoven's estate evidenced his friend's unswerving faith in him. After those of his brother Johann, Gerhard and Stephan von Breuning have the most entries in the dying composer's last conversation books.

In ample compensation for Breuning's naive reliance on Schindler (and occasionally on Rochlitz) his *Memories of Beethoven* provides us with a host of significant and unique materials, observed by an intelligent eyewitness, honestly recalled, and painstakingly presented. For the earlier years, Breuning's personal observations are enriched by family traditions, especially by information obtained from his father, such as the striking picture of the adolescent Beethoven trying to shield his father from arrest for disorderly behavior, and a rendering of the composer's reaction to Breuning's report of brother Caspar Carl's dishonesty. Gerhard von Breuning's interviews with several of Beethoven's contemporaries yielded valuable results – Grillparzer's outraged reaction to Beethoven accepting "charity" from the Philharmonic Society; Katherina Fröhlich's recollection of Beethoven's agitation during a keyboard improvisation when she was a little girl: "... his expression became so wild that I began to be afraid and tried to leave," but Beethoven signalled her to stay and tried to calm her by playing more quietly. Through Breuning we obtain rare insights into homely details of Beethoven's eccentricities at home and on the street: how he would "spit on the mirror, instead of out the window, without noticing the difference"; his impulse to retaliate when he was taunted by street urchins; how he would strip to his underclothing when walking through the Vienna woods; all of these illuminated by Grillparzer's wonderful remark, which Breuning preserved: "Despite all these absurdities, there was something so touching and ennobling about him that one could not help admiring him and feeling drawn to him." Breuning appreciably furthered our understanding of the aging Beethoven's personality; and his first-hand reports of the composer's last months – the atmosphere of the sick-room, the course of the medical treatment, his visitors, the death throes – are a permanent contribution to the Beethoven literature. And precisely because he had such strong likes and dislikes, his character portraits are clearly etched, and we will long remember his caustic descriptions of Dr. Wawruch showing off his Latin and of brother Johann reclining in his carriage like a patrician, as well as the affecting image of Beethoven, despairing of his doctor and of his life, muttering "Oh, that ass!" as he turned his face to the wall.

Stephan von Breuning died suddenly on June 4, 1827, barely two months after Beethoven's funeral; he had been ill with a liver condition and suffered a relapse following the first auction of Beethoven's personal effects. Gerhard believed that his father sacrificed his life for his friend, and indeed, Beethoven's final illness and the responsibilities of the guardianship, coming at a time of great stress in the elder Breuning's professional career, doubtless had overtaxed him. After his father's death, Gerhard was raised by an uncle, Josef Ritter von Vering, and educated in Vienna, where he attended the Gymnasium, enrolled as a student of medicine at the Josephinian Military

Academy, and was graduated as a doctor of medicine on April 13, 1837. At first he worked as a military doctor, but from 1852 he devoted himself exclusively to private practice.

Over the years, having come to realize the importance of his connection with Beethoven, and in preparation for his book, he began to make contact with the leading Beethoven scholars. He corresponded with Wegeler in 1845;[29] visited Schindler; became acquainted with Thayer, who furnished him with various documents, including private communications from Karl Holz. In later years, he was also in contact with Kalischer, Nohl, and Frimmel. The latter recalled how Breuning "not unwillingly made a display of his Beethoven reminiscences and customarily was to be seen at concerts where Beethoven's works were performed."[30] In addition to the present book he published three related papers – an essay on Beethoven's and Schubert's skulls, a series of extracts from the conversation books (mostly of conversations with Grillparzer and Holz), and an article containing the first publication of three Beethoven letters.[31] He died in Vienna on May 6, 1892, at the age of seventy-eight.

ı►✦◄ı

Breuning's own notes have been retained as footnotes. Substantive corrections of Breuning's text are to be found in the numbered annotations – given as endnotes – which also serve to identify persons or objects mentioned, amplify events described, clarify obscurities, and call attention to debatable issues. Wherever found, simple errors and repetitions in Breuning's internal bibliographical citations have been silently corrected or expanded, and cross-references to English-language editions provided. Similarly, errors in spelling of proper names or transcriptions of documents have either been silently corrected or explained in the notes.

ACKNOWLEDGMENTS

For information, assistance, and copies of rare materials I am grateful to Dr. Grita Herre of the Deutsche Staatsbibliothek Berlin; to Dr. Robert Kittler and Dr. Walter Wieser of the Österreichische Nationalbibliothek; and to the helpful staffs of the New York Public Library and the Libraries of Columbia University. Illustrations from the collections of the Beethovenhaus in Bonn, the H. C. Bodmer Collection of the Beethovenhaus, the Gesellschaft der Musikfreunde, and the Österreichische Nationalbibliothek are reproduced with the kind permission of those respective institutions. Material from the unpublished Conversation Books of Beethoven is quoted by permission of the Deutscher Verlag für Musik, Leipzig. I am especially grateful to my editor Penny Souster of Cambridge University Press for her confidence in this edition and for her numerous excellent suggestions; thanks also to copy-editor Mary Richards for seeing the manuscript through the press. The translation of the poem by Gabriel Seidl on pp. 110–11 is by James Day. The illustrations were photographed by Maury Solomon. This edition is dedicated to the memories of my friends Max Serbin and Gladys Schwarz.

Gerhard von Breuning, *Aus dem Schwarzspanierhause*, first edition,
Vienna, 1874, title-page

Aus dem

Schwarzspanierhause.

Erinnerungen

an

L. van Beethoven aus meiner Jugendzeit.

Von

Dr. Gerhard von Breuning.

Mit einem bisher unveröffentlichten Portrait-Medaillon Beethoven's nach Harneman
vom Jahre 1802 und einer Ansicht des Schwarzspanierhauses.

Wien 1874.
Verlag von L. Rosner.

In loving memory of my children
Gerhard, Constanze and Emma,
to whom I told these stories and
to whom I dedicated them.

Ah, it seemed impossible that I should leave the world
before I had produced everything I felt within me.

Beethoven, Heiligenstadt Testament
October 6, 1802

❦

Nature wants only life, no matter how or what
    She only operates with large amounts
    And paints us as she likes, either big
    Or just an empty zero, as she counts.
      Past and gone!

Friedrich Halm, "Dahin"

PREFACE

Several times over the years I had started to set down my memories of the time I had spent with Beethoven, and the things I had heard from my father, who died shortly after Beethoven; but somehow, putting these bits together was a task that was always postponed.

And so the anniversary year of 1870 approached, and it became more urgent than ever for me to carry out my undertaking; but this time too I was prevented from doing so. – On March 11 of that year death took from me my younger son, at the beginning of his nineteenth year, just as his spirit was fully unfolding.

Thereafter, the hundredth anniversary of Beethoven's birth was splendidly celebrated in Vienna; and the following year, in Bonn, the same event was marked by stirring performances of Beethoven's masterpieces, applauded by the Titan's admirers, who had assembled from all over the world.

I had received the following invitation to the Bonn festival:

Bonn, July 8, 1871.

Dear Sir:

Last year the respectfully undersigned Committee had the honor of inviting you to the projected celebration of the hundredth anniversary of Beethoven's birth. Unfortunately, the celebration could not be held because of the sudden outbreak of the war. We have now decided, after the gloriously achieved peace, to proceed with the celebration, with the same program as was scheduled for last year (the exact days are given on the enclosed brochure) and we have the honor herewith to renew our invitation of last year. We should attach great value to your kind acceptance of our invitation, since it would be a particular attraction at a Beethoven festival to have persons present among the guests of honor who were, directly or indirectly, personally close to the great hero in whose honor the celebration is being held. It would be an added pleasure for us in view of the fact that it was in the house of your honored family here in Bonn that the first rays of light illuminated the somber youth of young Beethoven.

We remain, very respectfully, in the hope of a gracious acceptance,

The most obedient Festival Committee

Chairman: Kaufmann, *Lord High Mayor*.

This most flattering invitation and charming attitude on the part of the Bonn festival committee could not but convince me that a personal account of the relationship of my forebears and myself to Beethoven would not be without interest to many people, and in fact that I had a sort of obligation to publish an account of my involvement with Beethoven, in view of the rare privilege I had had of being so close to that genius, and in view of the friendly invitation of the Bonn festival committee. Completing the manuscript and seeing it through the press has been delayed until now because other occupations repeatedly intervened.

If the information published here is able to hold the reader's lively interest, it will have achieved its purpose and I shall be happy; but in any event these lines will attest that Wegeler spoke the truth in his Supplement (*Nachtrag*) when he said: "Beethoven's memory lives on in the (Breuning) family."[1]

DR. VON BREUNING

Vienna, Summer 1874

In August 1825 I had the good fortune, during an afternoon walk with my parents, to make the acquaintance of Beethoven. – We were walking along the avenue that encircles the inner city of Vienna and cuts across its Glacis, and were between the Kärntner and Caroline gates. My father was about to turn off into the Caroline gate to go to his office when we saw a man walking alone, heading straight towards us. No sooner had we caught sight of one another, than there were the most joyful of greetings on both sides.

He was powerful-looking, of medium height, vigorous in his gait and in his lively movements, his clothing far from elegant or conventional; and there was something about him overall that did not fit into any classification.

He spoke almost without pause, asking how we were, what we were doing now, about relatives on the Rhine, and many other matters, and, without taking much time to wait for my father to answer why he had not visited him for so long etc., he said that he had lived in the Kothgasse some time ago and more recently in the Krugerstrasse; he joyfully hastened to tell us that soon, at the end of September, he would be a close neighbor of ours, in the Schwarzspanier house (we lived diagonally opposite in Prince Esterházy's Rothes Haus),[2] a piece of information that aroused considerable interest; he then hoped we would see a great deal of one another; he asked my mother to take those occasions to put his very disorderly housekeeping arrangements in order once for all, and keep an eye on them thereafter; and so forth. My father seldom got a chance to put a word in, but when he did, always spoke astonishingly loudly and distinctly, gesticulating animatedly, and with heartfelt assurances that they could and would soon be able to get together, he took his leave for today.

My desire to meet Beethoven, which I had so often expressed to my father and mother, had been satisfied at last. Now, with youthful impatience, I counted the days until I came into the close contact that I longed for with the famous friend of my father's youth, who had so often been mentioned to me.

For some years Beethoven and my father had met only infrequently. At first there had been a rather serious disagreement (see pp. 52–3); then, after reconciliation, each had been so busy with so many things that it was not easy to pick up their former relaxed relationship, especially since Beethoven's frequent changes of address and his way of life, which was so irregular in many respects, made it hard to put into effect the oft-repeated desire to look him up and find him. Despite these interruptions, however, relations between them remained the same as they had been since they were boys

PLATE I   Gerhard von Breuning in 1825, aged 12.
Unsigned lithograph miniature

together,* and – now I will go back, in order to give the reader as much acquaintance with family life in the house of my father's parents, which was so important for Beethoven, as is needed for fuller understanding.

ᴵᴺᵉᴰᶜᴬᴴ

In my grandparents' house in Bonn, an old General, a close friend of the family, was an almost daily guest. This was Baron Ignaz de Cler, Governor of the city. Whether at breakfast time or in the evening, he always came as a word-of-mouth newspaper to tell of happenings in the city and news in general. Once, it was on January 13, 1777, he came into the room looking very disturbed and even more withdrawn than usual, and sat down meditating, with both hands on the handle of his cane. From his appearance, something unusual had taken place, and of course those present urged him to make known the causes for his disquiet.

"A strange report," he finally began, "reached me today. The sentry on duty in the court of the Buenretiro from 12.00 to 1.00 at night had to be taken to the infirmary. His relief found the poor fellow unconscious. At the guardhouse he reported, and again this morning before my adjutant: as soon as he had taken up his position, he noticed that the sky, which up till then had been murky, was getting lighter. It became clearer and clearer at one point of the firmament above the palace, until a fiery rain poured onto the palace, coming from the gap in the clouds. This shower of sparks lasted a good ten minutes, without catching alight. Then, however, it got dark around him again, and the gap in the clouds closed up. But then the clouds parted once more, and he clearly saw, against the blue background of the sky, a large elegant coffin, with seven smaller and poorer ones around it. At this apparition he was so terrified that he fell unconscious."

"That is my coffin," said my grandfather, Emanuel Josef von Breuning,[4] in a very strange manner, when the General had finished his story. Those present gazed at one another in astonishment at this statement, as unexpected as it was peculiar, and although people tried to convince both my grandfather and themselves that the remark was without foundation, the group could not rid itself of a certain dejection, and it broke up less cheerfully than usual.

---

* Beethoven wrote to Wegeler on Oct. 7, 1826[3] (see Wegeler and Ries, p. 49; Eng. edn., p. 48): "I remember all the love which you have always shown me; ... likewise all the kindnesses I have received from the Breuning family. If we separated, that happened in the natural course of things; everyone must pursue his destined goal and try to attain it. But the eternal, unshakable foundations of goodness remained and always bound us together ... "

PLATE 2   The Breuning family in Bonn. Unsigned silhouette, 1782

Two days later, on January 15, a destructive fire broke out in the part of the Elector's palace occupied by the municipality, which in addition to many works of art also contained archives and offices. Upon hearing the news, my grandfather, who lived nearby on the Münsterplatz, hurried there to save the most important documents from his office, where he served as Electoral Court Councillor. Twice he succeeded in carrying loads of documents from the burning room with his own hands, and on a third trip he had already reached the palace gate when a burning beam crashed down on him and broke his spine. He died the next day, after hours of torturing pain. He had been born on October 11, 1740, and was only thirty-six. Seven workers also died in the blaze. – The vision of the sentry and my grandfather's pre-monition had both come true. However, the fire had been stopped at St. Florian's chapel, as it had in 1689, and the Buenretiro, sheltered by it, was spared in 1777 as well.

This "strange story, confirmed by the most reliable of testimony" was told by Christian von Stramberg, perhaps in somewhat embroidered manner, in his *Denkwürdiger und nützlicher Rheinischer Antiquarius, Mittelrhein*, part 1, vol. IV (Coblenz, 1856), pp. 116–118. The story was related in connection with a picture of St. Agatha, who is particularly honored in the Rhineland as a protectress against fire, for the same reason that "St. Florian's name is held in high esteem, since he proved his effectiveness not only in 1689 but for a second time in 1777 in saving the St. Florian chapel and the part of the palace abutting onto it."

Denkwürdiger und nützlicher

Rheinischer Antiquarius,

welcher die

wichtigsten und angenehmsten geographischen, historischen
und politischen

Merkwürdigkeiten

des ganzen

Rheinstroms,

von seinem Ausflusse in das Meer bis zu seinem Ursprunge
dargestellt.

Von einem

Nachforscher in historischen Dingen.

———

Mittelrhein.

Der I. Abtheilung 4. Band.

———◆◆◆———

Coblenz, 1856.
Druck und Verlag von Rud. Friedr. Hergt.

PLATE 3   *Denkwürdiger und nützlicher Rheinischer Antiquarius,*
Coblenz, 1856, title-page

PLATE 4   Helene von Breuning and her sons, Christof and Stephan.
Miniature portraits by Gerhard von Kügelgen

Thus, the chapel and Buenretiro were saved and the destructive force of
the fire was turned away from them, while my grandfather and the seven
workmen died in the catastrophe.

I have repeatedly heard the story, as I have told it here, from relatives. A
Count Hatzfeld that my father happened to meet in the antechamber of
Imperial Chancellor Prince Metternich, many years later, still remembered
the catastrophe.[5] He had himself seen the eight bodies on their biers, and he
still recalled the sensation the event had caused in Bonn at that time.

Naturally, the sudden loss of a father at the age of thirty-six would mean a
complete change in the circumstances of any family, and so it was for us,
despite the family's affluence.*

The Court Councillor's widow Helene von Breuning, daughter of
Electoral Physician Stephan Kerich, was then only twenty-six; her children
were:

Christof, born May 13, 1771 in Bonn;

Eleonore Brigitte, born there April 23, 1772;

Stephan (my father), usually called "Steffen," in Bonn, on August 17, 1774,[†]
    followed by

Lorenz, "Lenz" for short, after his father's death, therefore posthumously.[7]

* I deliberately emphasize this because of the fact that the "Bonn" author of the festival play
  "Ludwig van Beethoven, ein Schauspiel," etc., inaccurately and unjustifiably has the
  daughter, Eleonore, speak repeatedly of poverty in the home of her parents.[6]
† Heribert Rau (in his novel *Beethoven*) and Wolfgang Müller von Königswinter (in "Furioso,"
  in *Westermann's Monatsheften*) incorrectly speak of Stephan as the older brother and Christof
  as the younger one. G. Mensch (in his *Charakterbild: L. v. Beethoven*, Leipzig, 1871) wrongly
  calls Christof Christian.[8]

The widow remained in the family house in Bonn until 1815, except for some intermittent prolonged or brief sojourns with her brother-in-law in Kerpen (a village between Cologne and Aachen) or with her sister Margarethe von Stockhausen in Beul an der Ahr (now the spa Neuenahr). The house is still there, with its window gratings and the cardinal's hat over the doorway to commemorate its builder, Cardinal Barmann; it is on the Münsterplatz, to the left of the cold statue of hard metal whose prototype, with his warmly-beating heart and gentle spirit, went daily in and out of the house that had become like home to him.[9]

A brother of my grandfather, Johann Lorenz von Breuning, a canon in Neuss (always known in the family as the "Neuss uncle"), moved to Bonn at once to take charge of educating the four infant children and, as head of the family of his dead brother, to take care of the family's affairs, which he did until his death in Bonn in 1796, at the age of 58.

There was still another brother of the deceased who had an influential place in the family. This was the brother-in-law in Kerpen mentioned above, Johann Philipp von Breuning, born in Mergentheim in 1742 and a priest from 1769, who soon thereafter went to Kerpen as a canon and died there on June 12, 1832. He was a very clever and extremely kind man; up to the time of his death, his house was the favorite playground all summer for the entire family and its friends, sometimes including Beethoven, who often played the organ in the church there.

Our first years of childhood and school were spent under this quasi-paternal control, amid the affection of uncles, aunts, and others.

This, in sketchy outline, was the situation of the Breuning family in Bonn at that time.

Children bring playmates, schoolchildren bring schoolmates home with them. With the years, the previously narrow family circle in my grandmother's house was enlarged from outside, and the ennobling influence of that virtuous woman was extended not only to her own children but to others as well. Once the child's heart and spirit have been well and solidly formed in his parents' house, he will make friends – false impressions aside – only with those of like temper.

The charming and ambitious character of a poor student soon made him a daily companion in the house. This was Franz Gerhard Wegeler, the son of an Alsatian burgher, who experienced the craving for knowledge early in his life, in order to break the bonds of his family's poverty and become what he did become, for himself, his family, and his contemporaries.[10]

PLATE 5   Franz Gerhard Wegeler. Unsigned lithograph

In 1782, when already a denizen of the house, he had met the son of a musician of the Elector's court orchestra,* still a boy rather than a young man, as devoted to the Muse of harmony as Wegeler was to learning and art, and already an excellent performer on the keyboard.

Eleonore and Lenz needed a piano teacher; Wegeler's young friend needed to give lessons to help support himself and his parents. In this way young Ludwig van Beethoven was introduced into the hospitable home of my grandmother. He soon became fond of her and she became a second mother to him, working in many ways to soften the sometimes headstrong nature of his character.† The children gained an eternal friend in him; in them he won friends who never forgot him.

Thus, as the children grew up and the home circle was enlarged by bright young people from outside, activity in the house became livelier and livelier, all the more so because all the young people in the house were animated by a general thirst for knowledge, inspired by the widespread literary reforms of the time.

Wegeler, the oldest of the young friends (he was born in Bonn on August 22, 1765, which makes him closest in age to Beethoven, who was baptized in Bonn on December 17, 1770‡), and the three sons of Court Councillor Breuning's widow were students; Wegeler and Lenz later devoting themselves to medicine, Christof and Stephan to law. Eleonore and even more so Lenz already played the piano well; Stephan and Beethoven took lessons on the violin together from Franz Ries, the father of Ferdinand Ries – later a student of Beethoven's and a composer; of Hubert Ries, for many years concert master in Berlin, whom I met again as a guest of honor at the Bonn jubilee celebration; of Josef Ries of London; of Josef Franz Ries, the Vienna piano maker, etc.[14]

Concerning the anecdote about a spider which is found in the earlier bio-

---

* Wegeler's meeting Beethoven on the peak of the Drachenfels, as related by Wolfgang Müller in his "Furioso," seems to be a romantic invention.

† "She knew how to keep the insects off the flowers," Beethoven wrote later, in gratitude.[11] Otherwise, there might have been serious danger to Ludwig's character and educational development, exposed as he was exclusively to the relationships and influences of his father's house, which were troubling in many ways.

‡ I say baptized, rather than born. Wegeler for the first time disclosed Beethoven's actual birthplace, and A. W. Thayer was the first to establish the true year of birth. The date of birth is still not precisely known.[12]

At my last visit to Bonn (August 1871), I found the address of the birthplace changed from 515 Bonngasse to 20 Kölngasse;[13] but the address was all that was changed, and the garret where Beethoven came into the world is still there, cramped as ever, to the left on the first floor of the courtyard.

graphies,[15] I never heard anything either from my father or Wegeler or anyone else. It tells that in Bonn, young Ludwig, who was an excellent violinist, shared his room with a spider who got so accustomed to his playing that it would always creep close by until it was slain by the odious blow of a strange hand. A. Schindler, in his biography of Beethoven, already called the story fiction. What my father did say repeatedly – and he played the violin correctly, though not perfectly, all his life, and was a judge of violinists – was that, as a youngster, Ludwig soon became a tremendous pianist but never had any particular purity of tone on the fiddle nor any outstanding ability on it; he was always likely to play out of tune, even before his hearing began to be affected; thereafter, of course, his violin playing was increasingly out of tune, until deafness made him give it up completely (see Wegeler–Ries, p. 119; Eng. edn., p. 106).

During the joint lessons with my father under Franz Ries, Beethoven played on an instrument from the Schwarzwald region, which he presented to my father at the end of the course of instruction as a memento and which I keep as a precious keepsake, along with an old-fashioned violin case that my father got from Maestro Ries at the same time. – Amongst an assortment of violin music of that period, my father also owned Fiorillo's *Caprices*.[16] On the title page was a picture of a little man playing the violin. Later, in Vienna, Beethoven in his capricious way said to my father: "This little man is far too small to master such difficult exercises."

Yet another art came to be represented in the house in Bonn, when the circle of family and friends was enriched by a pair of doubly interesting brothers. These were the von Kügelgens, later well known as painters,* attractive twins, who soon joined our intimate family circle and became our fast friends.[17] My father claimed these boys were so much alike that for a long time no one could tell them apart, and my grandmother, in whose house they were now daily guests, put ribbons of different colors on them. It was only later that a gradually increasing difference in their personalities could be observed.

Karl von Kügelgen became a landscape painter† and in time went to St Petersburg. Gerhard von Kügelgen, who had a great gift for painting classical subjects and portraits, met a fate similar to Winckelmann's tragic

---

* F. Ch. A. Hasse, *Das Leben Gerhard's v. Kügelgen. Nebst einigen Nachrichten aus dem Leben des k. russischen Cabinetsmalers Karl v. Kügelgen* (Leipzig, 1824). Further, Wilhelm von Kügelgen's agreeably written *Jugenderinnerungen eines alten Mannes*, 3rd edn. (Berlin, 1871).

† He is represented in the Imperial Art Gallery in Vienna.

end.[18] In his forty-eighth year (March 27, 1820) he was murdered on the highway near Dresden. I have various works by him, from my father's estate, including splendid medallion likenesses of my grandmother, of my father in 1790, and others.

Thus, irrevocably the years of youth passed, in blithe association and thorough study of science and art, in gay social life, often enhanced by many a delightful visit by relatives and neighboring friends, and reinforced by many chance encounters, which occurred more frequently perhaps in those days. For time and place often influence people's spirits, and it is not always nor everywhere possible to find such gifted and ambitious young people together as must have been the case in the relaxed and easy-going house of my grandmother.

But even at that time the center of animated interest was young Beethoven, whose improvisations roamed over the piano of the house half the night through.*

However the dark thread that the Fates had woven into Beethoven's life had already begun to appear intermittently. His young friends, so sensitive and so sympathetic, were deeply moved, my father told me, by young Ludwig's sorrows and actions when his father, all too fond of wine, was disorderly on the street at night and got into trouble with the police. With a child's love and devotion (dedicated mainly to his long-suffering mother, it is true) he got between his father and the night watch, in a conflicting mixture of childlike love and civic duty. In those cases he would defend his father desperately to keep him from the disgrace of going to jail, even though that made him guilty of resisting the police patrol. His friends would then intervene to smooth matters over, to console, to protect, using the influence of their respected families; and this must have made a lasting impression, a lifelong one. Beethoven never forgot what they had meant to him, in what a spirit they had helped him at fateful moments in his life.

Except for his mother and his grandfather, who had a warm place in his heart, his relationships with his family caused him many a sorrow from the beginning of his life to its end. Nonetheless, his youth had its bright and agreeable moments.

There are some familiar stories that have often been told: his early dedications to the art-loving Elector Max Friedrich, the worthy brother of

---

* The music room on the ground floor, left, is still where it was. The present owner, Herr Gerhard, has only replaced the house's green wooden shutters with iron ones and some of the windows have been enlarged.

Westermann's
Illustrirte Deutsche Monatshefte.

Nro. 49.   October 1860.

Furioso.
Novelle von Wolfgang Müller von Königswinter.

Erstes Capitel.

An einem schönen warmen Junitage des Jahres 1785 ging durch den tiefen Wiesengrund des Siebengebirges, der sich von Königswinter nach dem Oelberge zieht, ein hochgewachsener schlanker junger Mann in jener Kleidung der damaligen Zeit, welche den und in der Dose aufsteckte, bald fing er einen Käfer, dem er in dem Fläschchen den Tod gab, um ihn später seiner Sammlung einzuverleiben. Man sah sofort, daß der junge Mann der Naturforschung ergeben war.

So emsig der Student nun auch seinen Beschäftigungen oblag, und so bedachtsam

PLATE 6   Wolfgang Müller von Königswinter, *Furioso*, illustration from first serial publication, in *Westermann's Illustrirte Deutsche Monatshefte* for October 1860

Emperor Joseph II;[19] his appointment, at an early age, to the post of electoral Court Organist on the recommendation of his first patron, Count Wald-stein;[20] Waldstein's many kind gifts to him; the mischievous incident with the tenor Heller, with whom he made a bet that he could throw him off pitch during divine service in the court chapel, which he succeeded in doing to his delight and satisfaction, to be sure with a "very gracious rebuke" from the Elector;[21] the joyful summer vacation with the Breuning family at "uncle's" in Kerpen, where he loved to play the organ in the village church; his merry trip with the Elector's court from Bonn to Mergentheim; his infatuations with Fräulein Babette Koch (later Countess Belderbusch) and (like Stephan) with Jeanette d' Honrath – later the wife of Austrian Lieutenant Field Marshal von Greth – whom I saw in Vienna in the twenties as an elderly lady (there was nothing more between Eleonore and Beethoven than a warm and permanent link of friendship, which among other things led to his choosing *Leonore* as the initial title of his opera[22]); his meeting with Josef Haydn as the composer was returning from England;[23] and so forth. These are told very charmingly, for those who like to read such stories with a little poetical ornament added, in Wolfgang Müller's "Furioso"; and told very truthfully in Wegeler and Ries' *Biographische Notizen* and in Schindler's biography of Beethoven and, with full references to conditions at the time, in A. W. Thayer's *Ludwig van Beethoven's Leben* (Berlin, 1866).

But time has wings, everywhere, not only with the aged, and the good times pass, alas, everywhere and for everyone. As the years go by, the seriousness of life begins to make itself felt.

So it was with our youthful little band. Wegeler went to Vienna in September 1787 as a medical student, in order to perfect himself for practical life in the brilliant medical school flourishing there under Joseph II. Christof and Stephan, the older sons, went to Göttingen to finish their law studies. Beethoven was sent to Vienna by his Elector, to the flourishing musical city where Haydn and Mozart were creating and performing things previously unheard of. All of these young people planned to leave their beloved homeland and their dear ones for only a short time. But it was a separation, the first one they had undergone, and it took place during the pressure of military events, during which delivery of mail by post chaise, limping along even in peace time, was sometimes completely interrupted.

But everyone's heart beat stronger, the further they went on the road towards fulfillment of their hopes and wishes.

Beethoven had come to Vienna in the winter of 1786–1787, and was

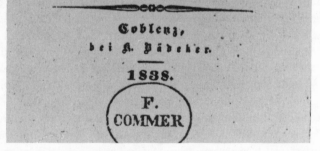

Biographische Notizen

über

Ludwig van Beethoven

von

Dr. F. G. Wegeler,

Königlich Preußischem Geheimem- und Regierungs-Medicinal-Rath;
Inhaber des eisernen Kreuzes a. w. B.; Ritter des rothen Adler-
Ordens III. Klasse mit der Schleife; Mitglied der medicinischen
Gesellschaften in Wien, Paris, Berlin, Bonn u. m. a.;

und

Ferdinand Ries,

Mitglied der Königlich Schwedischen Akademie, der Kaiserlich-
Oesterreichischen u. Königl. Holländischen Musik-Vereine.

(Mit dem Schattenriß des sechszehnjährigen Beethoven
und mit lithographirten Brieffragmenten.)

Coblenz,

bei K. Bädeker.

1838.

F.
COMMER

PLATE 7   F. G. Wegeler and Ferdinand Ries,
Biographische Notizen über Ludwig van Beethoven,
first edition, Coblenz, 1838, title-page

received everywhere with open arms, given the most courteous of receptions by the great art-loving aristocratic families of the Vienna of that time.[24] Wegeler too had come there in 1787, armed with a very warm recommendation and support by the Elector and, like Beethoven, had doors opened for him among the circle of the famous professors and physicians of the era of Joseph II: Brambilla, Gerhard von Vering, Gottfried van Swieten, Hunczovsky, Adam Schmidt and many others;[25] and who could have failed to be surprised and delighted at experiencing the magnificent talent of the exuberantly developing Beethoven, of whom even at that time the greatest genius of music had pronounced the prophetic words: "Watch him, he is going to make a name for himself in the world."[26]

Beethoven came back home to Bonn once more. This was because of his mother's illness, which soon lead to her death from consumption on July 17, 1787, in her forty-ninth year.[27] – Soon, however, the closely-knit circle of friends was to be separated again, never to reunite. The occupations of the various youths cast them out into the world.

The two Kügelgens were sent on a traveling fellowship by the Elector (May 4, 1791) with a "yearly stipend of 200 ducats for 3 years, so that they may try to perfect their fine gifts further in Rome."[28]

Then, early in November 1792,* came Beethoven's second trip to Vienna which became his permanent home. He never saw his native Rhine again, despite the fervent wishes to return he expressed in his letters to Wegeler and Eleonore. He did not return even when Eleonore married Wegeler on March 28, 1802.

F. G. Wegeler received his doctor's degree in Vienna on September 1, 1789 and returned to Bonn to begin his medical career as practising physician and professor. He was soon much in demand in Bonn and its environs. From October 1794 to June 1796, he had another period of happy association with his Ludwig in Vienna. On his return to Bonn his respected position enabled him to seek the hand of Eleonore. In 1807 he moved to Coblenz, where he lived an active life as Privy Governmental and Medical Councillor until his death (May 7, 1848; Eleonore died before him on June 13, 1841), keeping an open house and remaining in close contact with the Ries family, father and

---

* In Beethoven's album (now the property of the Imperial Court Library in Vienna), published by G. Nottebohm (*Beethoveniana, Aufsätze und Mittheilungen*, Leipzig and Winterthur, 1872), in which his childhood friends wrote during the last days of his stay in Bonn (October 24, 1792 onwards), Widow Koch dated the leaf she wrote on, "Bonn, Nov. 1, 1792, on the last evening before our parting."[29]

sons – especially Ferdinand – and many other interesting personalities,* and maintaining an intimate correspondence with Beethoven.

Christof von Breuning became professor of law in Bonn, then a government official in Cologne, and in later years Privy Superior Appeals Councillor at the Supreme Court in Berlin, the position he held when I met him in Berlin in 1838. Shortly after retiring, he died on his estate at Beul an der Ahr, where he is buried.

Helene von Breuning, the widow of the Court Councillor, moved to Cologne about 1823 or 1824, to her son Christof, and later to Coblenz to her son-in-law Wegeler, where I saw her in the fall of 1838. In her last few years, however, her memory had become so feeble with age† that she kept confusing where she was living at the time, and the people around her, with other people and other places. She died on December 9, 1838, a few weeks after my visit, having been a widow for sixty-one years.

Lenz von Breuning studied medicine and went to Vienna with Wegeler in 1794. There he profited once more from Beethoven's instruction and often made music with him at my father's musical evenings, which the Hunczovsky family also attended.[31] Lenz returned to Bonn from this instructional trip and died there, aged only twenty-one, on April 10, 1798. At that time Brownianism was the latest thing in medicine.[32] He was a "most intimate" friend of Beethoven's, as my father often said. Lenz's album had the following page:

> The truth exists for the wise,
> Beauty for a feeling heart!
> They belong to one another.
>
> Dear, good Breuning!

Never shall I forget the time I spent with you in Bonn and here. Continue to be my friend and you also will find me ever the same.

Vienna, October 1, 1797.
Your true friend
L. v. Beethoven[33]

---

* Zelter tells, in his Goethe letters (*Briefwechsel zwischen Goethe und Zelter*, vol. III, p. 335), what a pleasant ride he had in 1823 in the diligence next to the "merry doctor from Coblenz," who starting at the Elbe (near Magdeburg) "tapped a barrel of anecdotes that kept running until he arrived at Hildesheim."[30] This is told by Wegeler's son, Dr. Julius Wegeler, in the biography of his father on the occasion of the fiftieth anniversary of his doctorate (Coblenz, 1839).

† My friend Thayer reports in his *Ludwig van Beethoven's Leben*, II, p. 170; (Thayer–Krehbiel, I, p. 94) that "in 1837–1838 Dr. Wegeler, Frau von Breuning and Franz Ries, all equally venerable in age and in character, sat together and talked of the events of 1785–1788"; but Grand-

The album is owned by Dr. Julius Wegeler. In connection with the word "Bonn," F. G. Wegeler (Wegeler–Ries, Supplement, p. 20; Eng. edn., p. 56) remarks hastily and quite incorrectly: "Lenz von Breuning, the youngest of the three brothers, was the closest in age to Beethoven." The fact is quite the contrary. Beethoven was five months older than the oldest of the Breuning brothers and almost seven years older than the youngest one. Yet, although Lenz was the youngest, and thus furthest removed in age from Beethoven, it is Lenz who feels called upon to write to Wegeler in January 1796: "Incidentally, he (Beethoven) is extremely attached to me."[34] This and the other facts given above, especially my father's statement, also cited, which I distinctly remember, all weaken Thayer's assumption in saying of my father (as the middle one of the three brothers) and Beethoven: "The two ... may have become acquainted in 1785 or 1786, but it was a factor working against any deep intimacy that there was an age difference of four years, one being still a schoolboy, a child among children, while the other was already an organist and composer, in the habit of moving among men."[35] At best, this is based on a subjective inference. Wegeler (Wegeler–Ries, pp. 44–45; Eng. edn., p. 44) says of my father, "He was the only one that had all the qualities to become a biographer of Beethoven. He was closely connected with him from the age of ten down to his death, with short interruptions."

And so Lenz early departed from the group, and forever; but none of these people ever saw Beethoven again.

Stephan von Breuning was the only exception. In many ways his fate resembled that of Ludwig. He was born in the same city, only four years later. He came to Vienna to live there permanently. They shared the same quarters for a long time. The two lost sight of one another for a time, in the pressure of the circumstances of life. Then, as chance would have it, shortly before their deaths, brought on too early by vexations, in Beethoven's case arising from his family, in Stephan's from his official duties, they found themselves close neighbors (Schwarzspanierhaus and Rothes Haus) and so could enjoy each other's company for a short time to their hearts' content; but then they went to their graves which were only a few steps apart*[36] in the same churchyard, within two months and nine days of one another, one mourned by the world, the other by his family and all those who knew him.

---

mother Breuning must be left out of these discussions because of the condition mentioned, at least during her last years.

* Stephan and his second wife, my mother, are in the v. Vering family vault in the Währinger Cemetery, in the same row in which Beethoven lies a few graves further up.

PLATE 8   Stephan von Breuning. Unsigned lithograph

At the beginning of his career, Stephan was attached to the Teutonic Order in Mergentheim. After seven years he, like many Rhinelanders, under the leadership of their countryman Fassbender, was taken into the Court Military Council in Vienna,* where he advanced rapidly by working unusually hard, so that as early as 1818, at the age of forty-four, he became a Court Councillor; such exacting zeal, combined with personally irritating and disagreeable incidents under the chairmanship of Prince Hohenzollern, led to his all too early death from sensitive nerves on June 4, 1827, when he was not yet fifty-three.

Stephan was introduced to Chief Field Physician Gerhard von Vering[37] in Vienna by a letter of recommendation from Wegeler and (about 1800), through Wegeler's recommendation, found Beethoven already at home there. Beethoven was soon still more at home in the quarters of his Stephan in the Rothes Haus.[38] There they both lived for a short time. After Beethoven moved, they still had their noonday meal together. A letter of Stephan's to Wegeler from Vienna dated November 13, 1804, relates this, but also reports Beethoven's trouble with his hearing, which had begun four years earlier and was increasing to an alarming extent. Since this letter is very significant, it is reprinted here (from Wegeler–Ries, Supplement, p. 10; Eng. edn. p. 149). To excuse his long silence, Stephan writes:

He who has been my friend from youth is often largely to blame that I am compelled to neglect the absent ones. You cannot conceive, my dear Wegeler, what an indescribable, I might say, fearful effect the gradual loss of his hearing has had upon him. Think of the feeling of being unhappy in one of such violent temperament; in addition reserve, mistrust, often towards his best friends, in many things want of decision! For the greater part, with only an occasional exception when he gives free vent to his feelings on the spur of the moment, association with him demands a real effort, to which one can never resign oneself. From May until the beginning of this month we lived in the same house, and right from the start I took him into my rooms. He had scarcely come before he became severely, almost dangerously ill, and this was followed by an intermittent fever. [His predisposition to liver trouble thus had already manifested itself.] Worry and the care of him used me rather severely. Now he is completely well again. He lives on the Ramparts,† I in one of the newly built houses of Prince Esterházy in front of the Alser barracks, and as I am keeping house he eats with me every day.[39]

---

* Stephan did not seek Austrian service, as Mensch (p. 96) states erroneously; the date is also given incorrectly.

† In the house of Baron Pasqualati, Mölkerbastei, now No. 8. My father told me that Beethoven liked this house because of its open view and airiness, and lived there on several occasions. The fact that he left it, nevertheless, was due to the usual reason: his absent-mindedness and disregard for external considerations which were always landing him in conflicts with neighbors, janitors and, in the end, landlords. For example, the following incident occurred in this

Thus far my father's letter.

Stephan began to be more and more captivated by Vering's daughter, who was then developing musically and in other artistic ways, and although he had great difficulty in tearing himself away from Bonn when he revisited it in 1807, we soon find him back in Vienna, a happy bridegroom, singing Julie's virtues and charms in many poems (which I possess).[41]

Julie was a pupil of Johann Schenk, the composer of *Der Dorfbarbier*, *Die Weinlese*, and so on (I still see his image, in breeches and short jacket over his frock coat).[42] She was a good pianist and even tried her hand at little compositions (which I still have). It was natural that Beethoven was doubly interested in Stephan's eighteen-year-old wife, and we see him, as with Lenz a few years earlier, not only playing four hands with Julie but showing his appreciation of her artistic efforts by dedicating to "Julie von Breuning, née von Wering" (correctly, Vering) his own arrangements for piano solo of the Violin Concerto (not a sonata, as Mensch states) Op. 61, first performed by Clement on December 23, 1806.[43]

Often, my father told me, Beethoven improvised for the young couple until deep into the night.*

house. Beethoven had quarters on the third floor, with a magnificent view over the Glacis and various suburbs, as far as Leopoldsberg and Kahlenberg, and to the right far beyond the Prater. In order to look out towards the Prater, however, he had to lean out over the window sill and turn his head to the right. His room was the last (easternmost) one on the fire wall and the next house was only two stories high at that time, so that the main wall of the house was unencumbered. If there were a window in that wall, Beethoven thought, the room would be a corner room, with a clear view in that direction as well! Getting that done seemed to him to be a simple matter, and he called in a mason. Whether it was the mason, the janitor or the landlord who objected to the demolition from the beginning or whether the mason actually started to break through (I seem to remember my father's saying that it was the latter), I cannot say; but when this work was abandoned, he gave notice at once, in high dudgeon over the unobliging attitude of the landlord, even though they were friends. But after a time he was enticed back into the same house by the splendid view and the accommodating invitation of his friend Pasqualati; further incidents of the same kind made him leave it again, and then come back, after another reconciliation. Finally, Pasqualati, in the expectation that Beethoven would return, is said to have left the apartment vacant for him for some time.[40]

* When one looks at the Brodmann grand piano (still in my possession), considered one of the best makes at that time, with its tiny tone and its mere five and a half octaves, one finds it hard to conceive how it could have been adequate for Beethoven's tempestuous improvisations, while realizing that it was as a consequence of Beethoven's sonatas that the piano was altered and strengthened into its present state, indeed it had to be almost made afresh. His gigantic piano sonatas must be regarded as inventions in a double sense, for he must already have had in mind the piano as perfected today, the piano of the future; and it would be fully justified to call the modern piano the Beethoven piano, as I seem to remember having read somewhere. – C. F. Pohl publishes some very interesting and artistically significant material on Beethoven's piano playing, in the *Jahresbericht des Conservatoriums der Gesellschaft der Musikfreunde in Wien* (1869-1870), taken from Carl Czerny's autobiography (which is a "previously unknown

But soon, on March 21, 1809, after only eleven months of marriage, Fate brought about a bitter sorrow. We see Stephan writing the epitaph for his beloved Julie:*

To the
Best of Wives,
Julie, née von Vering,
Stephan von Breuning,
Imperial Court War Secretary,
In Deep Mourning
Erected
This Monument
To Married Love.

She was born on November 26, 1791, blossomed into tender beauty, combined with a rare seriousness of character, the most delightful sense of truth and purity, all the virtues of gentle womanliness, the noblest of feelings for nature and art, and pure cultivation of the mind true in every way to the essence of womanhood.

She died on March 21, 1809,
in the eleventh month of a most happy marriage,
at the very moment of the coming of Spring.

ιא૭Ꮶᴑᴦ

manuscript" in the archives of the society).[44] Pohl says: Czerny compares Hummel's playing to Beethoven's in these words: "Beethoven's playing was incredibly powerful and full of character, marked by a matchless bravura and fluency; Hummel's playing was a model of the utmost purity and clarity, graceful elegance and distinction, and the difficulties were always calculated to produce the greatest, most admirable effect, as he combined the Mozartian manner with the Clementi method, so well adapted for the instrument.... Hummel's supporters accused Beethoven of abusing the piano, of having no clarity or purity, of using the pedal so much as to produce nothing but confused noise, of composing music that was contrived, unnatural, unmelodious and, into the bargain, clumsy. To this the Beethovenists answered that Hummel was wanting in any true imagination, his playing was as monotonous as a barrel organ, the way he held his fingers was like a spider, and his compositions were mere reworkings of themes by Mozart and Haydn." – Pohl adds the report of a correspondent to the *Allgemeine Musikalische Zeitung* from Vienna in April 1799 on Beethoven's playing: "Beethoven's playing is brilliant in the extreme, but not very delicate, and at times becomes unclear. He shows to the best advantage in free improvisation. There it is really remarkable to see with what ease, coupled with full development in the sequence of ideas, Beethoven takes the theme given him and not only varies the figures (which is the stock in trade of many a virtuoso) but really develops them. Since the death of Mozart, who for me still remains the *non plus ultra* in this respect, I have never experienced this kind of pleasure to the extent that I did with Beethoven."[45]

* Julie is at rest in the Währinger Cemetery, to the right, just opposite the "Mausoleum of the Vering Family." My son Franz also rests in her tomb, since March 14, 1870, torn from me so early, on March 11.[46]

"Spring came to life, so blooming so fair,
Alas! it found her no longer there;
Moments of joy, and ages of sorrow
Are the fate of the lovely, today and tomorrow."

My father remained in the Rothes Haus to the end of his life, and Beethoven was always in close contact with him. In 1811, for example, Stephan wrote to his mother, "I have written to Wegeler that I now have a household of my own, with a cook, 66 years old. Beethoven eats with me. When he is not here, as was the case all summer, and it is likely to be again soon, since he intends to go to Italy and then return, I eat alone."[47] – The trip in question never took place. However, Beethoven, despite his trouble with his hearing, which was already in an advanced state, took part in the quartets that were resumed at Stephan's on regular days of the week, and the two friends were frequently involved in musical undertakings. One instance was the negotiations Beethoven had in connection with the staging of his opera, and there were many other such occasions.[48]

My father wrote to his sister Eleonore and her husband (Wegeler–Ries, pp. 62–66; Eng. edn., p. 58–60):

Vienna, June 2, 1806.

Dear Sister, dear Wegeler,
... If I remember rightly, I promised in my last letter to write to you about Beethoven's opera. Since it certainly must be of interest to you, I'll keep this promise. The music couldn't be more perfect and beautiful, and the subject is interesting; it tells of the liberation of a prisoner through the loyalty and courage of his wife; but yet, for all that, nothing has caused Beethoven so much annoyance as this work, whose value will only be fully appreciated in the future. In the first place, it was given seven days after the French troops marched in; the moment couldn't have been more unfavourable. The theaters were empty, of course, and Beethoven, who also noticed that there were some things wrong with the way the text was treated, withdrew the opera after three performances. After life returned to normal, he and I took it up again.* I reworked the entire libretto for him,† making the action more lively and rapid; he made cuts in

---

* Ries tells us (Wegeler–Ries, pp. 103 ff; Eng. edn., p. 91), on the basis of information received from Röckel, the tenor, that "Beethoven's friends decided, after the lack of success in 1805, to cut the opera. To this end, they met at Prince Lichnowsky's; the group consisted of the Prince, the Princess (who took the piano part; she was well known as an accomplished performer), the (poet) Court Councillor von Collin, Stephan von Breuning, the last two of whom had already discussed the cuts, – and then Herr Meyer, the first bass, Herr Röckel, and Beethoven."

† The text for "Lydia's Faithlessness" is also by my father, translated "from the French," and I found the song that Beethoven composed to it, written out completely in my father's hand, in

many numbers, and thereafter it was given three times to tremendous applause.[49] However, there were enemies of his in the theater and he clashed with some of them, especially at the second performance, and they brought things to a point where the work was no longer given after that. Even earlier, many difficulties had been put in his way. A single example as evidence of these is the fact that at the second performance he could not get the announcement of the opera to be made with the revised title *Fidelio*, as it is given in the French original and as it appeared on the printed version after the changes had been made. In violation of all the promises made, the first title, *Leonore*, was found on the posters for the performances.[51] What made the intrigue all the more disagreeable for Beethoven was that he has been set back financially by non-performance of the opera, for which he was to be paid on the basis of a percentage of the receipts. It will take him all the longer to pull himself out of it because the treatment he has received has made him lose much of his desire to work and pleasure in working. I may have given him the greatest pleasure when, without his knowing anything about it, I had a little poem printed and given out in the theater, both in November and at the March production. I will copy them out here for Wegeler, because I know from the old days that he likes that sort of thing; and since I once wrote some verses for his appointment as *Rector magnificus celeberrimae universitatis Bonnensis* (Most Reverend Rector of the celebrated University of Bonn), he can now make the comparison and see whether my genius for occasional verse has made any progress. The first little poem was in blank verse:

> Our greetings to thee on a mightier road,
> Called by the voices of admirers loud,
> Since modesty has held thee back too long!
> As thou setst forth, the garland blooms on thee
> And older warriors welcome thee with joy.
>
> How mightily thy music's power works,
> It pours in flood, like to a brimming stream.
> In fair alliance, art and delight embrace;
> Since thou hast felt, thou touchest other hearts.
>
> Within our breasts we felt the fearful storm
> Of Leonore's courage, her love and tears;
> Her faithfulness resounds in joyful clang
> And woeful care gives way to happy ease.
> Go boldly on; to grandsons yet unborn,
> Enchanted by thy wondrous music's sound,
> The rise of Thebes will seem no more a tale.

my father's papers.[50] – I have this original and lent it to my uncle Wegeler to use for his Supplement.

The second poem* is in two stanzas and contains a reference to the presence of the French troops at the time of the first performance of the opera:

Greetings to thee once more upon the path
Thou troddest in the dreadful ways of fear
When sweet illusion's magic bond, by wrath
Was broke in two, and desolation drear
Seized upon all as, like a feeble lath,
A skiff is tossed by the storms in mad career,
Art fled in terror from harsh scenes of war.
Not sympathy evoked our tears, but gore.

Thy strong determined step fills us with pride.
Thy gaze, aimed only at the highest strand,
With art and sensibility allied.
But see! The fairest Muse's hand
Sheds wreaths on thee, and from the thicket's side
Apollo cuts the fragrant laurel band.
Long may it rest on thee! May thou express
In music ever true beauty's loveliness!

Making this copy has really tired me out, and it may be just as well for me to end this letter, which is already long enough. I will only inform you that Lichnowsky has sent the opera to the queen of Prussia and I hope that the performances in Berlin will show the Viennese what they have here.[53]

But despite every effort this magnificent opera was never able to hold the stage permanently, and it can truthfully be said that it was in the summer of 1859 that it first found deeper understanding and a permanent place in the repertory in the Vienna theater, when the German opera season ended with a performance of it, with Aloys Ander singing Florestan, and the new German season was opened with it, with the same cast.[54]

A music critic in London begins an extensive report by saying: "Court Councillor Stephan von Breuning's prediction, made 45 years ago, has now been brilliantly fulfilled by the really excellent production of this opera" in London in 1851. He adds (*Illustrated London News* and *Wiener Theaterzeitung*,

* The first poem was printed in octavo. The second one was on a half-sheet folded to quarto form and headed: "To Herr Ludwig van Beethoven, on the occasion of his opera, first given on November 20, 1805 and now repeated under the altered title of 'Leonore,'" (With the Gerold papers).[52]

June 1851): "The art-loving world of London has had a double delight in the last few days. Beethoven's *Fidelio* was given in Italian for the first time, in two theaters at the same time. Private and press reports compete in describing the brilliant success of the two performances of this 'most German of all German operas,' which are called the best of the season. Of the four overtures, the one in E was played before the curtain rose, the great *Leonore* overture in C before the third act, and the storm of *vivas* made it necessary to repeat both, as well as many other numbers. Balfe conducted in Her Majesty's Theatre; he replaced the spoken texts by recitative; Costa was the conductor in the Royal Italian Opera House. Both were rewarded with ovations. An idea of the beauty of the performance can be obtained from the fact that the chorus of prisoners was supported by such singers as Gardoni, Calzolari, Pardini, Poultier, Scotti, Ferranti, F. Lablache, Lorenzo and Massol, and that the solo parts were sung in the first-named theater by Mlle. Cruvelli, Mr. Sims Reeves, Balanchi, Coletti, etc., and in the other by Madame Castellan, Signori Tamberlik, Formès, Tagliafico, Stigelli, etc. A masterwork like this," the reviewer continued, "can only be properly given with master performers like these, and that is what happened." —[55]

My father's second wife was Constanze Ruschowitz, my mother. – To her too Beethoven was always very friendly, as he was to women in general, always feeling attracted to them. For a time, in fact, she got the impression that Beethoven would have liked to pay court to her. He evidently contrived to bump into her remarkably often when she was going somewhere and then walk along with her some of the way. Once, for instance, he accompanied her to the "Kaiserbad" on the Danube, where she was going for a swim, and she was more than a little surprised upon coming out, something more than an hour later, to find Beethoven still on the bench in front of the bath house, waiting to accompany her back to the Rothes Haus. And so forth, and so on. –[56] The truth is, however, that to make Beethoven happy it would have taken a woman with very special qualities of mind and heart, a woman that it would be hard but possible to find. It would have had to be a woman who understood his flights of genius; who, without encumbering his frequent downswings with additional burdens of everyday affairs, could lead him in a womanly way while protecting him against the heedless outside world and its assaults on him; a kind of "angel Leonore." – But although he was one of those "who have had the great good fortune of being friend to a friend," it is highly doubtful that he would have been one of those of whom it could be said, "He who has got a noble wife, let him join in with his rejoicing," although he could sing its praises so greatly in music.[57]

Beethoven's heart felt love's flames repeatedly, but with the honorable basic idea: "not until I am entitled to call you mine."

My mother once wondered out loud to my father how it was possible that Beethoven could be attractive to women, when he was neither handsome nor elegant, in fact was unkempt, even wild in appearance. My father answered, "And yet he was always successful with women." – There was always in Beethoven a noble elevated sensitivity, which women perceived, whether in relationships of friendship or of love. –

The period in Beethoven's life extending from the time when he began to be famous, down to his death, produced an enormous number of reports, anecdotes and incidents, often untrue or at best distorted; and especially so in view of the pronounced idiosyncrasy of his character. For example, the stories in the *Jugend-Album* (Stuttgart, 1859, p. 145), intended as romantic, are not only false but vulgar: "Four pictures from L. van Beethoven's childhood, by Emil Ohly: The Pomander; The Forget-me-not; Music and Rhine Wine; The Little Improviser." – Likewise totally invented are: "Beethoven Leaves His House for the Last Time" (*Presse*, Vienna, March 9, 1866); "Beethoven's Torn Shoe," by Cl. Jäger in *Haus* (*Fremdenblatt*, Vienna, June 24, 1870); and also entirely fictitious is everything written, in a popular, over-wrought style, in the *Illustrierte Welt*, vol. 19 (Stuttgart, 1871) in connection with the much-quoted saying, "Beethoven was never out of love." There is simply nothing correct at all in the entire article except the physical description of Beethoven, "His was a sturdy, thickset, strongly-built figure"; and even here the next phrase, "the unsightly red pockmarked round face framed by a mane of thick black hair," calls for correction in that his face was not at all red and pockmarked, but spotted here and there with brown smallpox depressions, as appears clearly in the mask of his face taken during his lifetime, in 1812.[58] –I am glad to confirm what is said about Beethoven "by a contemporary," in the same article: "As soon as his face became animated in friendship, it took on all the charm of childlike innocence; when he smiled, one believed not only in him, but in mankind; so heartfelt and sincere was he in words, in movements and in looks."[59] –

The truth about Beethoven's character is that he had these traits: great nobility and tenderness, with an easily excitable temperament, mistrust, withdrawal from the world around him, together with a penchant for sarcastic wit. We need not give any evidence here as to the nobility of his spirit;

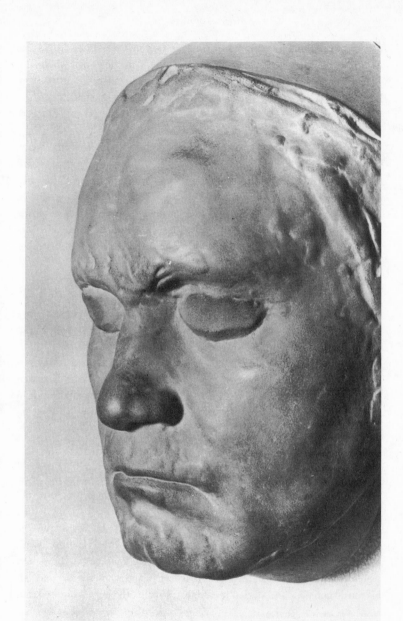

PLATE 9   Beethoven. Cast by Franz Klein, 1812. Unsigned photograph

a glance at the will he drew up in Heiligenstadt in 1802, a look at his frequently published letters, especially those to his nephew, his dealings in
general, all show how noble his mind was. His suspiciousness was based on
his dreadful deafness; his ready outbreaks of anger* were soon made good, in
the most amiable way,† by his quick admission, even to the point of exaggeration, of any mistakes he might have committed.

His withdrawal from the outer world sometimes showed itself in extreme
forms of behavior. For example, he would, without giving it a second
thought, take off practically all his clothes and carry them tied to his stick
over his shoulder, when the summer heat got to be too much for him during
his walks in lonely woods. He did this particularly in his favorite woods
between Baden and Gaden; so that my father several times voiced his fears
that there might be unpleasant incidents if he happened to encounter other
people.

His absent-mindedness almost caused him once to lose the entire receipts
of the benefit performance of his *Battle of Vittoria*.[61] He had carelessly thrust
the amount taken at the box office under his coat and then lost it on the Josefstädter Glacis. Fortunately, someone coming after him handed it to him after
picking it up; he accepted the package laconically (honesty was a matter of
course for him), did not make much of the matter and went on his way.

The incident with the manuscript of the Kyrie of his Mass in D is well
known. It went astray for some time while he was living in a country house in
Döbling. He was dismayed at the loss, but found it again, by chance, being
used as wrapping paper for butter, etc. in his kitchen; his cook apparently
regarded it as waste paper.[62]

Schindler has told us how Mödling Beethoven, during the composition of
the Credo for the same Mass, went without food for several days and once,
without being aware of it, came home without his hat, which the storm had
blown off his head.[63]

Here is another instance of his absentmindedness. He went into the
"Schwan" inn, which was near the "Mehlgrube" (now the Hotel Munsch),
with the idea of having his midday meal there. He knocked for the waiter,
who did not come at once; then he knocked again and while waiting took out
his music notebook and started to compose. Finally, the waiter inquired, but

---

* See Wegeler–Ries, pp. 129–132; Eng. edn., pp. 116–119. Beethoven's letters to Ferdinand
Ries about Stephan von Breuning, etc.
† See below Beethoven's letter of apology to Stephan von Breuning.
   Dr. Aloys Weissenbach offers "Characteristic Traits" of Beethoven in a most informative
manner, in Gustav Nottebohm's *Beethoveniana*.[60]

the deaf master was no longer aware of him. Since Beethoven was a steady customer, the waiter went off for the time being and Beethoven wrote for a long time, deep in thought, closed his book and asked for the bill, although he had not eaten anything.[64]

On the other hand, yet another exaggeration is the story that once, when Beethoven was living in the "Landstrasse" suburb, he went to the "Zum Rothen Hahn" restaurant there and, when the soft-boiled eggs he ordered arrived over-cooked, threw them at the waiter.[65] (A wineshop that Beethoven frequently visited at one time is the "Zur Stadt Triest" in the left corner house of Himmelpfort and Rauhensteingasse; also the "Jägerhorn" in the Dorotheengasse. However, he liked to wait to hear of the success of his chamber music compositions as performed by the Schuppanzigh quartet in a corner of the beer hall "Zum Igel" on the Wildpretmarkt, the rear house of the former hall of the Gesellschaft der Musikfreunde, which stood there until 1869.)[66]

The incidents mentioned above, which could be matched by many others, show how often Beethoven was totally withdrawn from his material surroundings. There are also abundant instances of the sarcastic humor that was one of his characteristics.

Grillparzer told me something about them (in the course of a visit to him in March 1860): "Beethoven always liked to be making jokes and playing tricks that went quite beyond normal social conventions. Sometimes this led to disagreeable situations and yet, despite all these absurdities, there was something so touching and ennobling about him that one could not help admiring him and feeling drawn to him. But he could only have close personal associations with friends who were aware of his true nature and had had evidence of his estimable qualities. Furthermore, it was very hard to make conversation with him. Apart from the fact that one always had to write, he would often skip from the subject to another one, while you were writing; then, in order to finish, you would have to remind him of what the topic had been, and that would often lead to confusion, and so forth. As a result, since for all his inadequacy for social life he always needed to have people about him, the only company he could have was either true friends, completely devoted to him, or else people who sought him out of self interest."

When Grillparzer expressed this opinion, I made reference to the fact that Schindler's enemies often accused him of being one of the latter group. This I did (because of my great respect for Schindler in contrast to what some of my acquaintances thought) in order to get Grillparzer's ideas on the matter; and he continued: "As for Schindler, I shall never forget how disconsolate he was when he informed me of Beethoven's impending death. When, a few days later, he notified me of Beethoven's death, it turned out that I was no longer as pleased with the funeral oration (at least, the last third of it) which I had written for Beethoven, because, instead of being so unprepared, I needed more time to write it; for I was too shattered by the news and when I am gripped deeply by something, I can no longer work well at it. This happened to me, for example, when I was describing Ottokar's grief over the corpse of his wife; suddenly I was so moved that tears came into my eyes. That is how it is with us: you have to feel the situation, be a part of it, and yet rise above it."[67]

Grillparzer told me of the following incident, as typical of Beethoven: "Once I visited Beethoven in his quarters: Ungargasse, near the Glacis.[68] He was standing at the piano and had his hands on the keys. When he saw me, he laughed and struck the keys mightily with both hands and left the piano. – Probably, the message he wanted to convey was: You thought I was going to play something for you, but I won't. – I didn't beg him."

Another incident he related to me indicated why he saw the matter in this light: "He and we, that is, my mother and I, shared the same house in Heiligenstadt;[69] he towards the street and we on the garden side, but we had the same vestibule and staircase. When he played, it was heard all over the house. In order to hear it better, my mother often opened the door to the kitchen, which was closer to his lodgings. Once she went out into the vestibule, by which I mean that part of it in front of the kitchen door, which was actually a part of our quarters. By chance, Beethoven happened to stop just at that moment and came out of his door into the corridor. When he saw my mother, he hurried back in, came out with his hat on and stormed out and – never played again all summer. It was of no avail for my mother to send her servant to tell him (he could still hear at that time) that she had only chanced to go out into the corridor, and not with the intention of listening to him. She even had the kitchen door blocked off. From now on no one was allowed to go through it up these stairs, but had to proceed to the garden and so out through the courtyard. – But he never played again."[70]

Grillparzer continued his recollections: "It was in Hetzendorf, in 1823 or 1824 if I remember rightly, that I had most to do with Beethoven. Once I visited him. There were no buses yet at that time, so I had taken a cab. When I started back to Vienna, he said he would like to come with me. I thought he just wanted to go part of the way, but he went along all the way to the Burg-thor. There he had the cab stop, got out and ran off like a madman, and when he was some way off, he laughed out loud and kept looking in my direction. I had no idea what it all meant, and then noticed a piece of paper folded up on the seat of the carriage. In it were six gulden in Viennese banknotes, the cab fare; and so that was what it was: he was delighted that he had outwitted me. – From anybody else, I should have taken such an act as an insult." (Both these stories have since been published in Grillparzer's collected works.)[71]

"Likewise," Grillparzer added, "I once dined at his house in Hetzendorf with Schindler. He brought five bottles of red wine out of the pantry: he put one in front of Schindler, one for himself, and three for me, as if to say: now you can drink all you want to!"[72]

Grillparzer blamed Beethoven in connection with the advance payment of £100 sterling he received from England in the last days of his life. When I touched on this matter in conversation with Grillparzer, in his characteristic frank manner, he expressed his predominantly patriotic opinion as follows: "He got support enough in Vienna not to need such a handout (and that was all those hundred pounds were, for they might have been giving him a pension). Archduke Rudolph, Prince Lichnowsky, and Prince Lobkowitz had promised him a pension, and they asked nothing in return, not even that he thank them or make courtesy calls, and – he afterwards did do just that, often enough.[73] – And yet," Grillparzer hastened to add, "for all his odd ways which, as I said, often bordered on being offensive, there was some-thing so inexpressibly touching and noble in him that one could not but esteem him and feel drawn to him," etc.

Katherina Fröhlich, the youngest of the three sisters of that name and widely known, by the way, as a friend of Franz Schubert's in his youth, in whose house (21 Spiegelgasse) Grillparzer lived in comfortable quarters from 1848 to his death, told me (likewise in March 1860): "Beethoven lived in my father's house in Döbling (on the left, mansion-like house next to Prof. v. Jäger's, the other side of the brook, in the courtyard, first floor).[74] When he was in a bad mood and nobody could go to him, I was often sent to him with the *Augsburger Allgemeine Zeitung* (his favorite reading matter); I was a little girl then. Most of the times he would smile at me, and sometimes he would sit down and start improvising. He would like to strike chords in F with his left hand and run up and down the keyboard with his right, making fantastic gestures. On one such occasion his expression became so wild that I began to be afraid and tried to leave. But he signalled me to stay, motioning me with his finger to sit down, and then went on playing with a little more restraint." –

There is an interesting episode, which I had known for several years previously, that was published for the first time by Eduard Hanslick (*Neue freie Presse*, 1870): "Beethoven as Messenger of Love." Ludwig Löwe was in Teplitz (Bohemia) in 1811 and had a love affair with Therese, the landlord's daughter. He always arrived after the other guests had left. Beethoven was at the same resort at that time and arrived later in order not to meet anyone, since he was already hard of hearing and for that reason hypochondriac. The girl's father discovered the affair and took Löwe to task, and Löwe kept away of his own free will, in order not to hurt the girl, with whom he was very much in love. After some time he met Beethoven in the Curgarten and Beethoven, who always had a liking for Löwe, asked him why he never came to the "Stern" any more. Löwe confided his secret and asked Beethoven whether he would take a note to Therese. In a spirit of friendship, Beethoven not only agreed to do so but offered to bring the answer back. In this way, the correspondence was carried on for some time. – Löwe does not know when Beethoven departed, but he himself went to Prague, after the lovers had plighted their troth; however a few weeks later he received news of his Therese's death. – In 1823 Löwe came to Vienna on tour, and visited Beethoven, who no longer remembered the happenings in Teplitz. When Löwe went on to tell him more about it, he was deeply interested in the story; and when Löwe said he was going to appear as a guest star, Beethoven replied that he would like to go to see Löwe in a play he was already familiar with, because he was already deaf. – That was the last time the two met.

I received very authentic confirmations, or partial corrections of my recollections of my life with Beethoven, in a final meeting with Anton Schindler, July 9 and 11, 1863, in Bockenheim near Frankfurt am Main (28 Hasengasse), where he lived during the last years of his life.[75] – Here are some excerpts from these conversations, which we both found very sad, held on several occasions and for hours, in sorrowful recall of days long gone by:

"It would seem that Beethoven could hardly deal with many persons in any other ways than in jest. For example, he always called Tobias Haslinger (formerly of the music firm of Steiner & Co.) "Adjutanterl," with special emphasis on the Viennese "erl," referring to his subordinate position under Steiner." (See below, Beethoven's letter to Haslinger concerning Clementi's piano method, and a similar one in Nottebohm's *Beethoveniana*.) At Schindler's I saw a canon that Beethoven had composed for Count Moritz Lichnowsky (in manuscript, of course), because of some advice that had not turned out well; if I am not mistaken, it dealt with a proposed public concert. The text of the canon runs: "Lieber Herr Graf, Sie sind ein Schaf (Dear Count, you are a sheep)."[76]

This delight in making jests, even of the most peculiar kind, on every possible occasion, is found very often in Beethoven. Thus, I found a sheet (a letter) in Beethoven's handwriting, with a laconic order in the lapidary style he often preferred, in ink. Under that was: "Datum, ohne zu geben (Date [= given], without giving)."[77]

A. W. Thayer showed me a letter of Beethoven's with the superscription: "Dear Holz (wood) of Christ's cross," and so forth and so on.[78]

I have another odd piece of Beethoven's writing. On a full-sized unfolded sketch leaf found on my father's desk, the entire length and breadth of the sheet is covered by writing in pencil:

> For Herr
> Court Secretary von Breuning.

On the other side of the same sheet:

> If you perchance
> On the Glacis today
> Should walk, you
> Would find me
> Between 4 and
> 5 o'clock.[79]

Schindler continued: "In the winter of 1822–1823 Beethoven lived at 61 Kothgasse (now 14 Gumperdorferstrasse), on the second floor, with a view of 20 Pfarr- (now Leimgruben-)gasse."[80] In this house he was very much put out by the rudeness of the janitor. There too he received the well-known New Year's greetings of his brother Johann, as "Landowner," which he answered at once by writing "Ludwig van Beethoven, Brainowner" on the back of the visiting card he had received.[81] "This was the period when he was working on the Ninth Symphony. From there he moved, at the beginning of summer, to Penzing, in the mansion-like house that is still standing (at this time 62 Parkgasse), by the footbridge (wooden in those days) across the stream of the Wien;[82] this house belonged to a tailor. Beethoven used to shave by the window in the morning and since it soon became known where he was staying, people using the bridge took the opportunity of watching him as he went about his business at the window. This began to get on his nerves, and when the people started stopping on the footbridge to stare at him, he decided to leave those quarters. – He immediately rented four rooms in Hetzendorf, in the lovely villa (now 32 Hauptstrasse) of Baron Pronay, for 100 Vienna gulden.[83] The Baron, who had enormous respect for Beethoven, had placed his spacious grounds at his disposal, and the only thing he asked was that Beethoven should not make any noise in the evening in the room of his that faced on the garden, because he himself slept, and very poorly, in the room below. At the start everything went very well. But since the Baron's enthusiastic veneration for Beethoven led him to make deep reverences every time they met, and Beethoven began to be aware of this, he began to feel ill at ease in the house. In order to bring the point home to the Baron, he tried to make himself as disagreeable as possible." From that time on he deliberately took his supper over the Baron's bedroom, and when Schindler, who had come to stay for some days, called his attention to the condition concerning that room, Beethoven started to make himself heard, drumming on the table with his fists, pushing the table to and fro, and so forth. Schindler did not approve of this behavior and finally left the room. The next morning he told Beethoven he wanted to return to Vienna; Beethoven merely answered, "Won't you have some coffee before you go?"[84] – Beethoven still disliked the continued compliments of his deferential landlord, and moved from this attractive dwelling to another one in Baden (94 Rathhausgasse) although a locksmith* was already living there. – "The upshot was that in that year Beethoven had four dwellings at the same time, and had started writing the Ninth Symphony as well!"[85]

For the subsequent winter of 1823–1824 he moved to Ungargasse, the left corner house at Bock-(now 5 Beatrix-)gasse, with a view on the latter;[86] in the summer of 1824 back to Baden; in the winter of 1824–1825 to 1009 Krugerstrasse (now 13), right of the stairs, second floor; in the summer of 1825, back in Baden, from which he moved in the fall to the Schwarzspanierhaus (Alservorstadt, old number 200, new 5), the last time he moved.[87]

Beethoven's brother's name was actually Caspar Carl, but he preferred to be called Carl, because it sounded better. – In this connection I mention the misunderstanding (see p. 19 above) that split Beethoven and my father once

---

* In his self-published brochure, communicated to the celebration of December 17, 1870, which gives everything that has or suggests a relationship of Beethoven to Baden, Dr. Hermann Rollett says that it was a coppersmith and not a locksmith (*Beethoven in Baden* [Baden bei Wien, 1871], p. 7).

again, and this time for a longer period and more seriously. Caspar Carl was a
government employee in Vienna, a cashier; his reputation was not of the best.
A friend of my father's, who learned of this, felt it was proper for my father
to know of it so that he might, without naming the source, on his word of
honor, warn Ludwig not to have any money dealings with his brother. My
father faithfully carried out the task he had undertaken. But Ludwig, in his
indefatigable effort to improve his brother, immediately hauled him over the
coals for his actions, reproaching him with all the accusations that had been
made against him of sordid behavior; he went so far, when his brother
pressed him for the source of the report, as to name his friend Stephan.
Caspar now went directly to my father and asked him for the name of the
author of the "denunciation," and when my father steadfastly refused to give
him the name (Rösgen), Caspar broke out in the lowest sort of abuse, going
to the point where he addressed libelous letters unsealed to the Imperial
Council of War for my father. My father, hurt and irritated by this
impudence and by Ludwig's breaking his word, gave Beethoven a sharp
rebuke ending with the statement that because of such unreliability he could
not associate with him any longer. The tension between the two friends
lasted a long time, until Ludwig wrote this incomparable letter of reconciliation:[88]

Behind this painting,* my good, dear St., may there be *hidden* forever what has *come
between us* for a while. I know, I have wounded *your heart*, but my own emotions,
which you must certainly have noticed, have punished me enough. It was not *malice*
towards you that was in my mind, no, I would never again have been worthy of your
friendship, it was passion *in you* and *in me* – but distrust of you was stirring in me. –
People came between us – who are never worthy of *you* and *me*; – my portrait was
intended for you long ago, you know that I always intended it for someone, to whom
could I give it with the warmest heart except you, true, good, noble Steffen – Forgive
me for hurting you; I suffered no less when I did not see you beside me for so
long, only then I felt keenly for the first time how dear you are to *my* heart and always
will be.

Your

(Undated and unsigned)

–Surely you will fly to my *arms* as *freely* as ever. –

(on the outside: "Pour M. de Breuning")

---

* This is the excellent miniature of Beethoven by Hornemann (1803), which I own and which is
published for the first time as an addition to this book.[89]

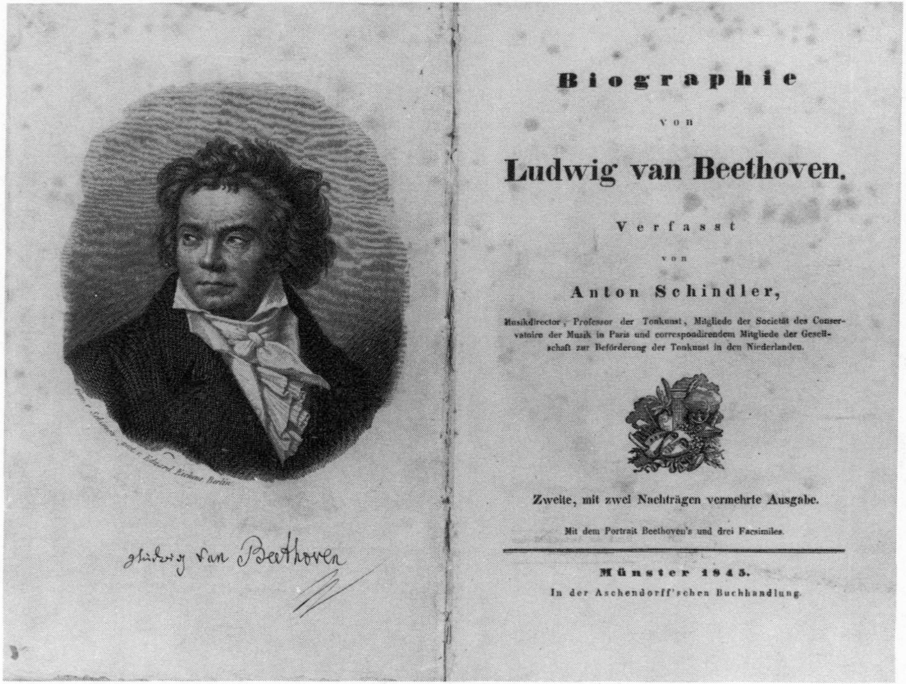

Biographie

von

Ludwig van Beethoven.

Verfasst

von

Anton Schindler,

Musikdirector, Professor der Tonkunst, Mitgliede der Societät des Conservatoire der Musik in Paris und correspondirendem Mitgliede der Gesellschaft zur Beförderung der Tonkunst in den Niederlanden.

Zweite, mit zwei Nachträgen vermehrte Ausgabe.

Mit dem Portrait Beethoven's und drei Facsimiles.

Münster 1845.

In der Aschendorff'schen Buchhandlung.

PLATE 10 Anton Schindler, *Biographie von Ludwig van Beethoven*, 2nd edition, Münster, 1845. Title-page with frontispiece engraved by Eduard Eichens after Beethoven's portrait in oils by Ferdinand Schimon

It goes without saying that such a heartfelt gesture led to complete reconciliation of the two friends, whose difference had arisen precisely from the nature of the situation.

Beethoven's brother's money troubles had unfortunately led Ludwig to borrow 2300 gulden from Frau von Brentano in Frankfurt am Main in 1810 or later, but it was not until 1823 that Ludwig repaid the debt. The kindness shown him in this matter led Beethoven to say on many occasions (as Schindler reports): that he had true friends only in Frankfurt.[90]

Other facts about Beethoven emerged from my conversations with Schindler.

"In 1803 I composed *Christ on the Mount of Olives* on one of these forked branches," Beethoven told Schindler, pointing to a tree with two stems coming up from the root, at the place where one goes left from the Hetzendorfer Gate of the Schönbrunn Garden towards the rotunda.[91] He could no longer find the exact tree because several similar ones had grown up since then. It must have been some time between 1817 and 1825 that he was there with Schindler.

On another occasion, when Beethoven went for a walk with Schindler along the Nussbach at Heiligenstadt, he pointed to a tree (now, since 1863, marked by the bronze bust by Fernkorn)* and said to him, "Here is where I composed the scene by the brook (Pastoral Symphony)." (More on this walk in Schindler, I, p. 154; Schindler–MacArdle, pp. 144–145.)

For the Tenth Symphony, which had already been started, there are some sketches in existence, including the theme of the first movement and the theme of the scherzo, the latter (to judge from what Schindler sang to me) probably like the theme of the first movement of the Fifth Symphony. On these sketches Beethoven had simply written: "X. Symphony." Schindler published them in the *Musikalischen-kritischen Repertorium für Musik* (Leipzig, 1824).[93]

Schlemmer was Beethoven's copyist for thirty years.[94] They were hard manuscripts to copy and few people could do justice to them. Schlemmer lived in the Graben, not far from the Kohlmarkt, in the rear part of a house. He had trained assistants, in particular one who worked for him for many years and, my mother told me, made his copies in a dark nailmaker's arch under the entrance gate to the Fischhof (then the Galvagnihof) on the Hoher Markt.

Among other matters I also asked about the story that Hummel, after

* Beethoven monument in Heiligenstadt near Vienna.[92] *Wien* (Zamarski and Ditmarsch, 1863).

promising the dying Beethoven to take part in Schindler's concert, had then refused (I think, unjustly) to go through with it, but in the end had performed.

It was completely characteristic that Schindler was taken aback when I reminded him of this incident, which he had left out of his Beethoven biography on purpose (Schindler, II, pp. 197–199; Schindler–MacArdle, pp. 389–390), and proceeded to tell me the following: "Well, since you still remember about that, I'll tell you what actually happened. It is true that Hummel, although in the middle of March he had promised Beethoven on his deathbed to take part in my concert on April 7, 1827, at the Josefstädter Theater, tried to back out of his promise after Beethoven had died. But Hummel's wife, born Röckel, still living as a widow in Weimar, was one loved by Beethoven; he wanted to marry her, but Hummel snatched her away from him. When she heard from me that her husband had changed his mind, she said, 'I have so much respect for Beethoven's memory that I will not permit this. Let my husband be; I promise you that he will play for you.' And in fact Hummel did play, and improvised on a theme of Beethoven's in the most beautiful way imaginable."[95]

I still remember the enthusiastic applause that Hummel received that evening from the public, still shaken by the death of Beethoven only a few days previously; I attended the concert with my father.

On this occasion Schindler showed me a considerable number of letters from Beethoven to him, in addition to letters from Meyerbeer, Humboldt, Unger, and others, as well as a package that Beethoven had tied up with twine and left behind, containing several printed opera librettos and manuscript librettos, as possible subjects for operas.*[96]

Moreover I saw in Schindler's possession, from Beethoven's personal effects, *The Odyssey* and Sturm's *Reflections on the Works of God in Nature*, 2 vols. (Reutlingen, 1811), with many holograph marginal markings and notes by Beethoven, partially cut off by the binder while Beethoven was still alive.[98]

I also found a letter from my mother to Schindler, in which she wrote that Hotschevar (the guardian of nephew Karl after my father's death) wanted to have certain papers handed over to him and that she was put in the position of defending Schindler against him.[99]

A special feeling, sad and joyous at the same time, came over me when I

---

* One of them was Grillparzer's *Melusine*, written expressly for Beethoven, who never set it to music; later, as we know, Conradin Kreutzer did write the opera.[97]

saw once more so many things that I have seen so often, in fact every day, in that long-vanished time: his cane, his heavy silver eyeglasses, his old-fashioned monocle with its cord, two brass seals with intertwined monograms LvB, the stem of one seal broken, two Cossack statuettes that he used as paperweights, a metal handbell standing on three feet, etc.[100]

Schindler intended to leave all those things to the Royal Library in Berlin after his death, "since the museum had already bought the majority of the conversation notebooks and was setting up a sort of Beethoven museum." In this connection Schindler remarked to me that the plan contemplated was to deny access to the Beethoven material collected in the Royal Library in Berlin until ten years had elapsed. (When I heard this, I could not help asking him to make an exception for me, for obvious reasons, in the case of any other objects in his possession that he might turn over in the future; Schindler consented at once.)

During my last visit to Schindler, he presented me with a music copy-book: a fragment of the A-major Trio from *Fidelio*, with corrections in Beethoven's hand: "I was glad to bring him refreshment, the poor man . . ."[101] – After this last visit of mine to Schindler in Bockenheim, I exchanged letters with him several times from Vienna. Before I received the promised note-book with the fragment from *Fidelio*, Schindler died, on January 16, 1864; he had been born in 1796 in Medl, Moravia.[102] However, his sister's son, Egloff,[103] handed it to me in Vienna shortly thereafter, in fulfillment of his uncle's promise. On the notebook I found, in Schindler's handwriting: "A. Schindler to Dr. Gerhard von Breuning as visible evidence of how Beethoven corrected his manuscripts." (See Schindler, II, p. 340; Schindler–MacArdle, p. 485).

ལ⊙☺⊙⋊⌇

And now cruel fate decreed that the great man, after so many changes of living quarters, should find his last dwelling, in association with friendly family and neighbors, filled with so many dear memories of youth, in the Schwarzspanierhaus, to which he moved for the fall quarter. He moved into this house on the Alservorstadt Glacis, old number 200, new number 5 Schwarzspaniergasse, between September 29 and October 12, 1825.[104]

If one were to calculate the duration of these events from the depth of our happiness one would have concluded that we were probably entitled to them to have lasted much longer. However, it was unfortunately written otherwise in the riddle-filled book of destiny.

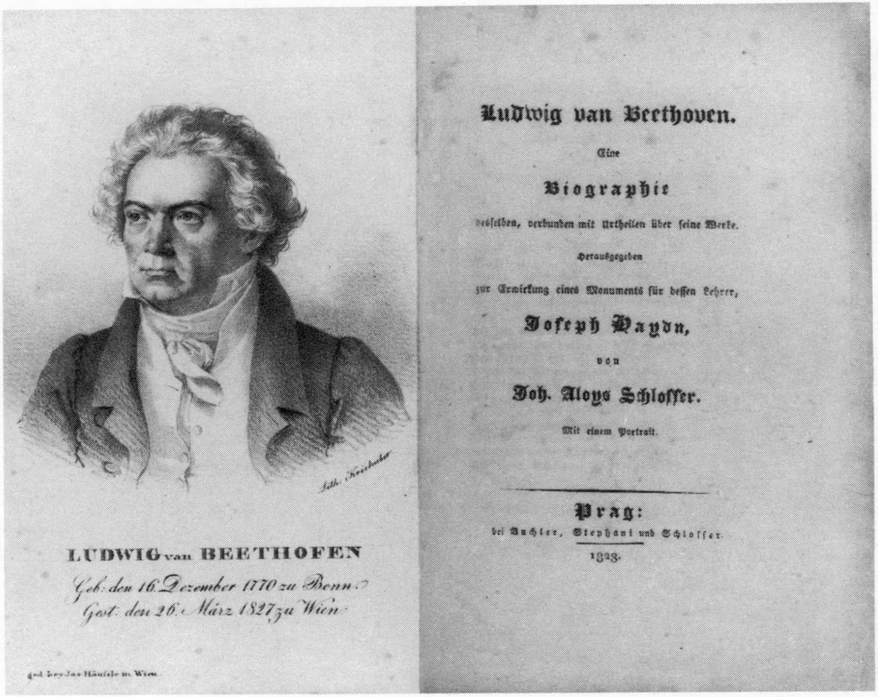

PLATE 11 Schlosser, *Ludwig van Beethoven: Eine Biographie*, first edition, Prague, 1828. Title-page, with frontispiece engraved from a lithograph by Josef Kriehuber after the drawing by Stefan Decker, 1824

PLATE 12   The Schwarzspanierhaus, exterior. Unsigned photograph

Our being such close neighbors led to a kind of community life that promised to bring my parents renewed youth, and for me was an exalted though all-too-brief episode of my childhood, all the more unexpected and deeply felt in that it ended so suddenly. Short as the episode was, its events penetrated all the more deeply into the mind of the ecstatic twelve-year-old boy; the hard blows of fate that ended it changed that boy's situation in life, but the impressions received during that happy period remained engraved on his memory.

Since then a flood of biographies, communications, and even anecdotes about this last period of Beethoven's life has appeared, and much of what has been told and disseminated has more imagination than truth in it. This I know from my recollections of that unforgettable time, from my looking into the conversation books, which I had known so well in the past, from my recent conversations with Schindler, etc. I shall therefore try to state what I remember from those days. I feel all the greater obligation to do so because it is precisely that last part of Beethoven's life that has been the subject of the most misinformation and inventions with no basis in fact, but I am the only person still alive of the few people around Beethoven during his last three months, the period of his last illness, and I saw him then for several hours every day.

Beethoven's having chanced to find quarters so near to where we lived was a source of great comfort to him too, and he had waited impatiently for moving time to come around. Now, at each of his visits, which were more numerous because of the arrangements involved in fixing up his new rooms, he would repeat the request he had made when we first met (see p. 19), that my mother should undertake to put his disordered housekeeping into some kind of system.

It was also a very attractive apartment. The Schwarzspanierhaus, on the Alservorstadt Glacis, facing south, was not at that time surrounded by any of the new buildings that have since been put up, and it had a wide view over the Glacis and the inner city lying just opposite, with its bastions and church towers, left to Leopoldvorstadt and beyond that over the towering trees of the Prater and the Brigittenau, towards the front over the extensive drill grounds of Josefstadt, the imperial stables, Mariahilfervorstadt and other suburbs; the only direction in which the view was cut off was to the right, blocked by the Rothes Haus, where we occupied quarters on the second story with ten windows to the right of the main entrance. The Schwarzspanier-haus, and the attached church, at that time used as a military bedding ware-house, had once been built by Benedictines from Spain, which led to an unusual arrangement of its windows.

In order to have the priests' living quarters higher, the middle bay of the house has only two stories in a series of nine windows, while on either side of this are three stories with four windows in each. However, the windows are so arranged that all the windows of the top floor are in a single unbroken row. Beethoven's windows were in this top (second story) row, beginning with the fifth (counting from the church) and ending with the ninth (the one beyond the main entrance).

The apartment was reached by the beautiful main staircase. It was entered by a simple, rather low door on the second story, to the left, opening on a spacious ante-chamber with a window (the one over the main entrance) looking out on the court. The kitchen and a large servants' room led directly out of this ante-chamber, all in all with four windows looking out on the court. The very spacious rectangular courtyard was formed by the structures of the building on three sides, and at that time was bounded at the back by the large garden, which has long since been sold for building lots. The houses thus erected form a street going in a straight line from the Lackirergässchen to the ante-chamber window spoken of above, and then ending, at a right angle, at the Garnisonsgasse up against the later-erected new building of the

PLATE 13   Entrance hall and door to Beethoven's apartment
in the Schwarzspanierhaus

General Hospital. The street was laid out in 1845. It was suggested to the
book dealer Dirnböck, as the most important property owner, that he give
his own name to the street, but with praiseworthy modesty he baptized it
Beethovengasse.

Wegeler (Wegeler–Ries, Supplement, p. 11; Eng. edn. p. 149, note) adds a
note at the word "Alser barracks," saying: "The recently built street, Beethovengasse, runs behind this house and the one Beethoven died in, named
after the black-robed Spaniards." This explanation, which is not accurate,
must be due to the fact that Wegeler was away from Vienna for 49 years.

Going to the left from the ante-chamber one enters a very spacious room
with a window on the street (the window over the door of the house), and left
from that to a similar room with one window. To the right of the entrance
room is a large room with two windows, and from that again one passes to a
large room with one window (this is the fifth window, counting from the
church) and a little door to the servant's room. These five windows look out
on the Glacis.

Light, warmth, spaciousness, proximity to my father, etc., made this

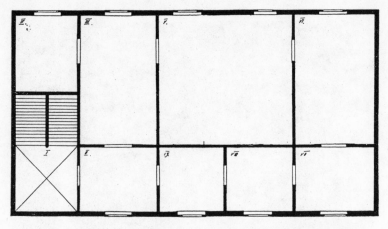

PLATE 14   Beethoven's apartment in the Schwarzspanierhaus. Ground plan

I   Staircase
II   Ante-chamber
III   Entrance hall
IV   Music room
V   Bedroom with pianos
VI   Composing room
VII   Servant's room
VIII   Housekeeping area
IX   Kitchen

dwelling a very agreeable one for Beethoven, who had longed for something just like that. I had known the apartment for some time, for at the beginning of the 1820s the same rooms, plus the now separate portion, with four or more windows extending up to the church, were occupied by Lieutenant Field Marshal Baron Minutillo,[105] whose sons were my playmates; I mention this to dispel the notion that the apartment was a poverty-stricken one. The apartment is still there as it was in Beethoven's time, except that the kitchen has been remodeled; and there it was on March 29, 1860, the thirty-third anniversary of the burial of the great departed one, that I entered the apartment, vacant at that time, with several friends (A. W. Thayer, Prof. and Mrs. Linzbauer,[106] Coroner and Mrs. Walther), and a few days later with my family.

The apartment was furnished in the following manner, in keeping with Beethoven's indifference to luxury:

As I remember it, the one-windowed ante-chamber had some chairs up against the wall, a simple dinner table, a credenza, and above it the half-length picture of his paternal grandfather Ludwig, of whom Beethoven was so fond (the picture is now in the possession of the widow of his nephew Karl).[107] The grandfather is shown in a green fur outfit, with a music notebook in his hand. This was the picture that at one time was in pawn in the tavern at Bonn, and was the only item from his parents' estate that Beethoven had sent on to Vienna. The one-windowed room to the left had no furniture, except the unused desk on the right by the window (this desk is now in my possession) and, on the end wall, just a large picture of Beethoven himself (the one with the lyre and the temple of the Galitzin hill; it is now owned by the widow of his nephew Karl, and A. W. Thayer has a copy, roughly contemporary).[108] On the floor, in disorder, were piles of music, engraved or manuscript, his own compositions and those of others. The room was hardly ever entered by anyone. I went in sometimes, out of curiosity or boredom or now and then because Beethoven had sent me in there to fetch something, and I would pick my way among the heaps of stuff. At my tender age I had no idea in those days of the treasures that were there; only half a year later, after Beethoven's death, how many manuscripts, some of them with still unpublished material, were scattered to the winds for a few gulden![109]

The two rooms to the right of the ante-chamber were Beethoven's actual living quarters. He slept and had his pianos in the first one, and the second was his study, where his last works were created (e.g., the Galitzin quartets).[110]

In the center of the first room, with two windows, were two pianos, set curve to curve. With the keyboard towards the door was the English piano that people from the London Philharmonic Society had once sent him as a gift. The names of the donors, among whom I remember Kalkbrenner, Moscheles and Broadwood, were written in ink on the sound board, under the soprano strings.[111] This piano, from the Broadwood factory, only went up to C.[112] On the other side, with the keyboard facing the door of the study, or composition room, was a grand piano from the Graf factory in Vienna, reaching up to F, lent to Beethoven to use.[113]* Above its keyboard and action was a sort of trumpet, like a prompter's box, made in the shape of a bent sound board of thin wood; the idea was to concentrate the sound waves of the instrument in the ears of the player. But I could see, one day in the summer of 1826, how hopeless the attempt was; this I shall relate later. Against the pillar between the windows was a chest of drawers; on top of that, up against

---

* In May 1866 the Supplement to the *Presse* gave the genealogy of a "piano of Beethoven's," from the factory of S. A. Vogel in Pesth, in the possession of Samuel Gyulai in Klausenburg (Belsö-Farkas-utcza 81). The very fact that it has "the splendidly worked coat of arms and clearly recognizable portrait of the young Beethoven" suggests that some admirer of Beethoven had this ornamented piano prepared for himself.[114]

PLATE 15   Beethoven's writing desk and memorabilia. Unsigned photograph

PLATE 16   Beethoven. Portrait in oils by Joseph Willibrord Mähler, 1804

the wall, was a four-shelf bookcase, painted black,* with books and papers; in front of it, on top of the chest of drawers, were several ear trumpets and two violins (erroneously described as Amatis).[116] All this was in disorder and hopelessly covered with dust. Beethoven's bed, a bedside table, a table and a clothes horse next to the stove completed the equipment of the room.

The last room (one-windowed) was Beethoven's work room. Here he sat at a table some distance from the window, just in front of the entrance door, with his face towards the door of the large room and the right side of his body towards the window. In this small room there was, along with other chests, the high, narrow and very simple bookcase or clothes chiffonier, once owned by Fräulein Annacker and now the property of A. W. Thayer.[117]

And so my mother had undertaken to organize the housekeeping arrangements. Her first task was to find him reliable help. A cook ("Sali") was found who turned out to be so devoted and reliable a person that as a faithful housekeeper and later also as a nurse she made Beethoven's house livable from then on to the end of his days.[118] This "Beethoven Sali" was provided with a kitchen maid to assist her, and the requisite kitchen equipment was purchased.

During this period of setting his household in order he got the idea of inviting us to have dinner with him, a project that he had long held out before us, and my father received the humorous, rhapsodical letter that is in my possession and was published by Wegeler (Wegeler–Ries, Supplement, p. 21; Eng. edn., pp. 157–158) with my permission, but incorrectly said to date "probably 1820":

You are overwhelmed with work my esteemed friend, and so am I. At the same time I am not yet quite well. I would already have invited you to dinner, but up to now I still need several people – of whom the most witty author is the cook and whose witty works are not to be found in their own cellars, but go into other people's kitchens and cellars; – whose society you would not profit by. But things are going to change soon. For the time being, don't get Czerny's piano method; I expect further information about another one any day.

Enclosed is the fashion journal promised to your wife, and something for your children. I can continue to send you the journal, and you are welcome to anything else you would like to have from me.

> With love and regards
> Your friend Beethoven
> I hope we shall meet soon[119]

---

* I still have it, cut down by two shelves. – The drawing of this room made after Beethoven's death (incorrectly captioned "Beethoven's study") shows this bookcase with four shelves, but of the two pianos, it shows only the English grand, and the wrong way round at that.[115] Beethoven's bust on the window is an addition of the artist's.

PLATE 17   Beethoven's study, Schwarzspanierhaus, with a view of the
St Stephan's church. Engraving by G. Leybold

(The number of the journal contained views of Switzerland: Lucerne, etc. Later he asked for it back for a short time; but then his sickness and death intervened and we lost track of it; it must have been lent to someone else.)

We see, from this letter, his almost idyllic hope for ease and comfort in his new quarters, things he had long been without. We also see how much he wanted company. He was not at all misanthropic, but from his own unfortunate experience he had good reason not to care for disagreeable company, whether strangers or relatives.

Although his household was now soon set in order, his rooms remained as disorderly as ever, dusty and with piles of accumulated papers and possessions, his clothes unbrushed despite the dazzling whiteness and cleanliness of his linen and his frequent bathing. This excessive bathing may well have been the original source of his hearing difficulty, perhaps by way of rheumatic inflammation, and may have caused his "predisposition to abdominal pains," as is frequently assumed. He always had the habit, when he had been at his desk for a long time composing, and felt that his head was overheated, of rushing over to the washstand and pouring jugfuls of water over his head and after cooling himself in this way and drying himself hastily, going back to work or taking a walk in the open air. All this was done in the greatest haste, in order not to lose his flow of ideas, and he paid no attention at all to properly drying his thick head of soaking wet hair. One thing that shows this is that, without his noticing it, the water he poured over his head would sometimes go all over the floor and even go through the ceiling to the floor below; this led occasionally to disagreeable situations with the people downstairs, the janitor, and finally the landlord, and even to having to move out. −[120]

My mother, like the orderly housekeeper she was, hated dusty plates and cutlery, and so forth, and had no particular desire to accept luncheon engagements under those circumstances, and tried to get out of his repeatedly expressed desire to invite us. She preferred to have him over to eat with us. This had the unfortunate effect that I never had the pleasure of observing a midday meal at his house, which would have been something interesting. On the other hand, he gladly accepted invitations to our house, or would often send us some fish when he had had some bought for him in the market. Fish was one of his favorite dishes and he liked to share things that he liked with friends.

When he had had lunch with us, and frequently on other occasions, he would go for a walk with us in the afternoon, especially on Sundays, since during the week my father could seldom take an afternoon off. It was a very

PLATE 18 Beethoven out walking.
Pencil drawing by Joseph Daniel Böhm
(c. 1820)

simple matter at that time to go for a walk, and we were all glad when now and then, instead of walking on the Glacis, which was all too familiar, we went along the Linienwall or to Herrnals and Ottakring, or even to Schönbrunn. – Since he soon saw how I was attached to my father and always kept close to him, he gave me the nickname of "Hosenknopf" ("trouser button," because I "stuck to him like a button on trousers."[121] But since I would always be running ahead of the group on these walks and then running back, and was always very lively, he later changed the name to Ariel, the name of the busy and sprightly messenger in Shakespeare's "Tempest." He held so steadfastly to these two names for me all through this period, even during his illness, that when he wrote little notes to me at our address in the Rothes Haus, they all began with one or other of these names. I received a total of twelve such notes, which I tightly bound with string, with information for me or my parents. Three of them began: "Dear Hosenknopf" and nine "Dear Ariel." Eleven of them were in pencil, only one in ink. To my eternal regret, they were thrown out as waste paper by some ignorant person when we moved after my father's death.

Because of Beethoven's remarkable indifference to the way he was dressed,

PLATE 19   The Breuning family: Stephan, Constanze, and their
three children. Unsigned portrait in oils

he cut a strange figure in the street. Usually buried in thought and grumbling to himself, he would often gesticulate with his arms when he was walking by himself. If he was walking with others, he spoke very loudly and vigorously and, since his companion would always have to write the answer in a conversation book, there were constant stops along the way, which in itself was striking and made still more so by the mimicry accompanying the answers.

As a result, passersby would usually turn around to look at him and the street urchins would add their comments and call out after him. His nephew Karl was ashamed to go out with him on this account and even told him on one occasion that he was ashamed to accompany him on the streets because of his "ridiculous appearance," which greatly grieved and wounded Beethoven, who told us about it. I, on the other hand, was very proud to be seen with such a prominent man.

At that time he wore the customary felt hat. When he came into the house, he would shake it a bit, even when it was dripping from the rain (a habit he practiced in our house as well, without concern for the furnishings of the room), and clap it down on the top of the coat stand. As a result, the top of the hat was no longer flat, but arched upwards. Whether before or after rain, it was seldom or never brushed and then got dusty again, so that it always looked frayed. Into the bargain, he tended to wear it pushed back from his face in order to leave his forehead free, while his disorderly hair, which Rellstab picturesquely calls "not curled, not stiff, but a mixture of everything,"[122] streamed out on either side. By putting on his hat and wearing it far back off the face, with his head held high, the back of the brim collided with the coat collar, which was worn very high at that time, giving the brim a permanent crimp, while the coat collar looked frayed from the constant rubbing against the brim. The two unbuttoned skirts of the overcoat, especially those of his blue frock coat with brass buttons, flapped out around his arms, especially when he was going against the wind; likewise, the two long ends of the white cravat around his broad shirt collar streamed outwards. The double lorgnette that he wore because of his short-sightedness, hung loose. The skirts of his coat were rather heavily weighed down. On one side there was his handkerchief, often hanging out, and on the other a rather thick music notebook in quarto format and folded together, plus an octavo conversation book and a thick carpenter's pencil,* these for communication

---

* Beethoven had a characteristic awkwardness in cutting the quills of his pens; similarly, his rather thick fingers were not very good at sharpening pencils without breaking them. This may have been why he liked to have thick pencils, like those carpenters use.[123]

with friends and acquaintances he met on the way; formerly, while it still helped, he used to carry an ear trumpet as well. The music notebook was so heavy that the skirt of the coat had stretched on that side; also, because the hand on that side was so frequently pulling out the music and conversation books, the pocket there was stretched outward. – The well-known pen-and-ink drawing reproduces Beethoven's figure pretty well, even if the hat was never tilted sideways, as the drawing (exaggerated, as usual) shows it.[124] – Beethoven's appearance, as sketched here, is indelibly impressed on my memory. I often saw him like that, from our windows, at about two o'clock (his dinner hour), in full sail homeward from the Schottenthor over the part of the Glacis where the Votivkirche now stands, with his body leaning forward (but not bent) and his head high, as usual, or I actually went with him myself.

Conversation with him was most difficult on the street, where there was not always time enough to write things down. That he was totally deaf was proved conclusively for me, if any such proof was needed, by the following occurrence. He was once expected for dinner with us, and it was getting close to two, our dinner time. My parents feared, with good reason, that he might have got deep into composing and forgotten all about the time, and sent me over to fetch him. I found him at his desk, facing the open door to the piano room, writing one of the last (Galitzin) quartets. He looked up and told me to wait a bit, until he had put his idea down on paper. I was quiet for a while and then went over to the Graf piano (with the added amplifying apparatus), which was nearest, and began to strum lightly on the keys, not being convinced that Beethoven was deaf to musical tones.* I kept looking in his direction to see whether he might be feeling bothered. When I saw that he was completely unaware of it, I played louder, and intentionally quite loudly; – and I had no more doubts. He heard nothing and kept on writing, unconcerned, until finally he was finished and came out with me. On the way he asked me something; I shouted the answer right into his ear, but he understood my signs more than my words. One time, though, at dinner in our house one of my sisters let out a high piercing shriek, and the fact that he had heard it after all made him so happy that he laughed out loud, showing his brilliant white full rows of teeth.

Another characteristic of his was the vehemence with which he would discuss subjects that interested him; and sometimes, as he walked up and

---

* Many people at that time, trying to be sophisticated, maintained that the great composer's hearing organs were deaf only to speech and general noise, but not to music.

PLATE 20   Johann van Beethoven. Portrait in oils by Leopold Gross

down the room in one of these discussions with my father, he would spit on the mirror, instead of out the window, without noticing the difference.

His life would now have been very pleasant, despite his deafness, to which, incidentally, he was fairly well reconciled by this time, had it not been for the way in which his brother Johann and particularly his nephew Karl continued to torment him. It would have been an easy matter, entirely within his power, to be free of both of them. Beethoven's brother was in comfortable circumstances; he owned a pharmacy in Linz, for the purchase of which my father stood surety at the time; through army contracts, etc., he became wealthy and lived on his income. The nephew did not require anything like the careful supervision that his uncle gave him so devotedly, partly out of love, and partly out of a feeling of what he thought was his duty to his dead brother. A person with a nature like Karl's gets through his inevitable process of growing up better if he is left to himself. After the death of his uncle and the end of his careful supervision, he left the army and became a quiet law-abiding citizen and decent husband and father. He died in Vienna April 13, 1858.

But Beethoven's blind love, the love with which he would have liked to embrace the whole world ("Be embraced, O ye millions, This kiss to all the world"), went too far here.[125] He never wearied, no matter how Karl's frivolous mother kept on interfering with his good influence. Once, on account of the boy, she entangled him in legal proceedings with the authorities that lasted for years. It can easily be understood that at that time the amount of creative work he could produce was seriously affected, and that in fact proved to be the case.

Every time he met my father, he would discuss his nephew, with anxious love: his worries over the results of the school tests; the way in which brother Johann and Karl's mother obstructed him at every turn, made his life miserable, etc. Other favorite subjects of conversation with my father were discussions of the artistic and financial success of his last two major works, the Ninth Symphony and the Mass in D; plans for future compositions, especially the form that he would or should give the tenth symphony he had in mind, "in order to create in it a new gravitational force," this time without a chorus; and also that he was sorry he had never gone to England, and that he never had married. Very often, too, the two friends plunged into reminiscences of the youth they had spent together.

In a word, our life was now a closely-linked neighborly one, filled with unfailing friendship and esteem.

IOHANN VAN BETHOFEN APOTHEKER ZUR KRONE

PLATE 21   Johann van Beethoven's apothecary shop, visiting card

I was still very shy; although I did not understand his greatness, I still felt it, and did not dare to make daily visits to him, as I wanted to. I was all the gladder, on that account, when he came to our house. He soon asked about my piano lessons and the name of my teacher, Anton Heller; Beethoven did not know him, and answered, "Hm, hm, alright." When my father assured him that the teacher was worthy but that I did not practice enough, Beethoven said: "Well, now, let him play something for me." I did so and he, without hearing a thing, looked very attentively at my hands, criticized the way I held them, and played a bit for me It was on the same Brodmann grand on which he had often played with Julie in the days long past and – at a time when he could hear – had improvised. – "What piano method has Gerhard got?" – Pleyel's. – "I'll get him Clementi's; it's still the best after all. Let him stick to that, and I'll advise him about what else to do." – The Clementi method was not to be had on the Vienna market. He had to have it ordered. –

In 1863 I found, at Schindler's in Bockenheim, in the package with opera librettos, a memorandum slip with notations in Beethoven's hand, the pencil writing already badly faded:

† mirror
† ducats
† flannel
† tailor
† soap for washing
† Breuning piano method

† at my brother's	† violin
busts of Handel, etc.	case
† wafers	today order
† flour	chamber pot[126]

(Schindler presented this slip to me, along with Beethoven's last laundry list.) – In October 1870 I found at A. W. Thayer's in Trieste a copy after Jahn of a letter* by Beethoven, likewise dealing with the matter of the piano method:

> To the noble
>   Mr. Tobias Haslinger
> formerly B.r.o.t. now art manufacturer,
> Dear Mr. North American music dealer as well as retailer!
> I am here for only half a day and ask you what the Clementi piano method costs, translated into German; please let me know at once, and whether you have it yourself, or where it can be found?
> Most excellent Sir, Hm, Hm, Hm! live well in your freshly varnished place of business, see to it that the former den is turned into a beer hall, because all beer-drinkers are good musicians and should order from you. Yours very truly
>
>   Beethoven[127]

It took a very long time for this Clementi piano method to arrive, but arrive it did at last, and he sent it over to my father from the Schwarzspanier-haus with the note that I let Wegeler have for publication in his Supplement. It runs:

> Dear Fellow!
> At last I can make good on my bragging. Here is the Clementi piano method for Gerhard that I promised. If he uses it in the way I am going to show him, it will certainly give him good results. I will be seeing you directly, and embrace you warmly.
>
>   Your Beethoven[128]

---

* My friend Thayer, with his usual willingness to oblige, has permitted me to publish it.

PLATE 22 Beethoven. Portrait in oils by Josef Carl Stieler, 1819–1820

In order that this letter should not be lost but remain as a lasting memento for me, my father sewed it into the piano method.

When Beethoven had shown me the above-mentioned scale on the keyboard, my mother and I were very eager to have him play something for us, or still better improvise. My mother and I had never heard him play. We appealed to father; but he could not abide the idea that Beethoven should play like an automaton without himself being able to hear what he was playing; he could not bring himself to remind Beethoven so palpably of his loss of hearing. And so this piano scale was the only thing I ever heard him play. He held his fingers very curved, so much so that they were completely hidden by the hand, what is called the old position, in brief, as contrasted to the present way, in which the fingers are characteristically more extended.

The sublimity of his improvisations is well known and would not have been impaired if he struck an occasional wrong note in leaps. (Julie's brother Dr. Josef von Vering, told me that once, at the Theater-an-der-Wien in the final days of Beethoven's public performances, Beethoven was playing one of his piano concertos while his hearing was already very poor, and kept on playing after several strings broke, without his noticing it). –

The first balloon ascent of Mme. Garnerin in Vienna was scheduled for August 28, 1826. She was to let herself down to earth by parachute from a dizzy height: a spectacle never yet seen in Vienna. Everyone was interested. But the day was also my thirteenth birthday, and Beethoven was invited to dinner for the celebration, and then after dinner to see from our windows, which looked over to the trees of the Prater, how Mme. Garnerin's new experiment turned out. He brought with him a copy of the Stieler portrait "with the Missa Solemnis,"[129] which M. Artaria had just published in lithograph; my father was to send it to Wegeler in Coblenz.* While we were waiting for the aeronautical performance to begin, comparisons were made of the similarity of the portrait to the original. My father's opinion was that although none of Beethoven's portraits was a perfect likeness, this one resembled him more than any of the other recent ones, especially if the small details are disregarded and it is viewed through the window from the back, so that its sharp outlines are softened. Beethoven was much pleased by this observation.†

---

* See Wegeler–Ries p. 53; Eng. edn. p. 51: Beethoven's letter to Wegeler, dated February 17, 1827.[130]

† Although the outlines of this first print were far too severe so that they occasioned the above remark, I must agree with Schindler (II, p. 290; Schindler–MacArdle, p. 453) that the latter print displayed by Spina is far too weak; I must also confirm that the inclined position

On September 24, 1826, my saint's day, Beethoven was once more our dinner guest, as was my tutor Waniek. Before dinner Beethoven showed us the gold medal he had received from Louis XVIII (now in the Archives of the Gesellschaft der Musikfreunde in Vienna).[132] During the meal he told us that the Vienna city authorities had given him the freedom of the city, and that someone had remarked that he had been given honorary but not genuine citizenship;[133] Beethoven had replied, "I hadn't known that Vienna had tainted citizens as well."

In the afternoon we all walked to Schönbrunn. My mother had a visit to make in Meidling (adjoining Schönbrunn). I accompanied her. My father, Beethoven, and my teacher waited for us on a bench on the lawn of the Schönbrunn garden. When we were walking in the garden later, Beethoven pointed to the avenues of trees pleached in the French style, and said: "All frippery, tricked up like the old crinolines. I am only at ease when I am in unspoiled nature." – An infantry soldier passed us. At once Beethoven was ready with a sarcastic remark: "A slave who has sold his freedom for five kreuzer a day."

As we were going homewards, a group of boys were playing skittles in the middle of the right-hand avenue in front of the Schönbrunn bridge, and the ball happened to hit Beethoven on the foot. Suspecting they had done it

of Beethoven's head was not characteristic of him.

   Among the other Beethoven portraits, the best likenesses are: the 1814 medallion portrait by Letronne, except for a tendency to give some of the features a mulatto-like expression; the portraits by Jäger, Chimon and Schiman (the latter in Schindler's biography); and especially, as my father repeatedly asserted, the miniature medallion portrait done in 1803 by Hornemann, which is the best likeness of all. It is in my possession and is published here for the first time. – The mask of Beethoven's face taken from life in 1812 by Johann Klein is remarkably true to nature. (The mold was then owned by the son of the painter Danhauser, and later came into the possession of the sculptor Anton Dietrich, who died in Vienna on April 27, 1872. – I own a very successful copy. – Streicher has a good bust. – Schaller's bust, which was not reproduced, was prepared at Karl Holz's initiative after Beethoven's death. It was purchased by Mrs. Fanni Linzbauer, née Tonsing, wife of the physician and a devoted admirer of Beethoven. On the occasion of the centennial celebration of Beethoven's birth, she presented it to the Philharmonic Society in London, in grateful recognition of the sum of money sent by the society during Beethoven's last illness. It was accepted by Mr. Cusins, the conductor of the Royal Philharmonic who made the trip from London to Ofen expressly for the purpose. (I possess a photographic copy of this.) – All the other portraits are more or less distorted or simply misdrawn.

   The recently published full length portrait of "Beethoven", with tight trousers, tasseled boots and pendent signet seals, is, by the way, that of an erstwhile Berlin painter, Wittich.

   Schindler says shrewdly that the best guide to choosing a portrait is the accurate picture of Beethoven's personality given by Friedrich Rochlitz (see his *Für Freunde der Tonkunst*, 4 vols. (Leipzig, 1824–32), IV, pp. 350 ff., and Schindler, II, p. 291; Schindler–MacArdle, pp. 454–455).[131]

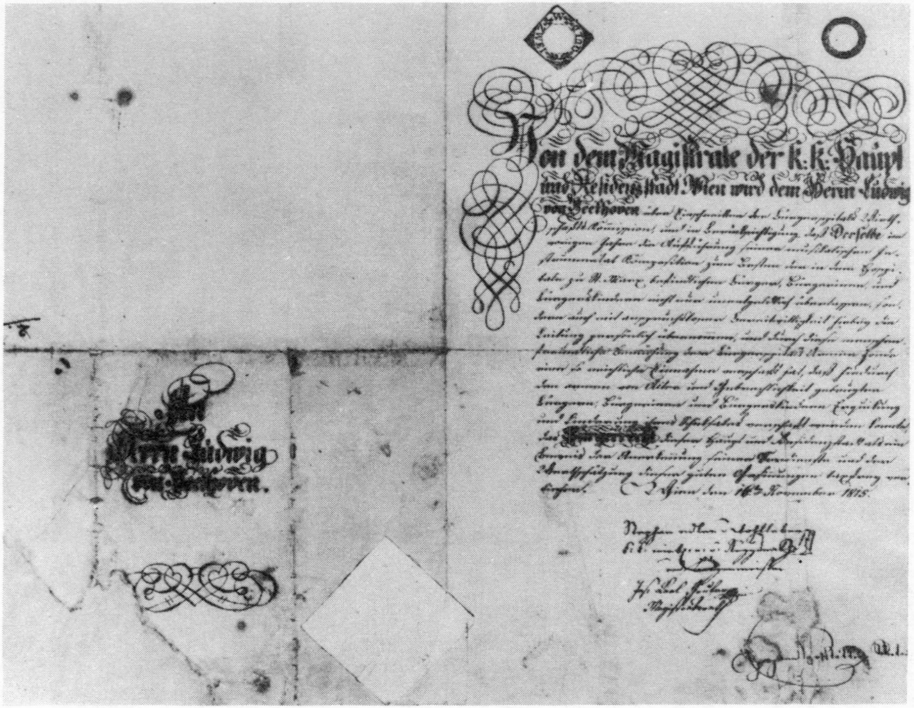
Von dem Magistrate der k: k: Haupt und Residenzstadt Wien wird dem Herrn Ludwig van Beethoven

Bürgerrecht

Wien den 16. November 1815

Herrn Ludwig van Beethoven.

PLATE 23 Beethoven's diploma of citizenship (Bürgerrechtsdiplom) from the Magistrat der Stadt Wien, 16 November 1815 intentionally in order to provoke him, he turned on them violently at once, shouting: "Who allowed you to play here? Do you have to do your mischief here?" He was about to rush at them to drive them away, but my father, fearing the toughness of the street urchins, soon calmed Beethoven down, and in any event the pain caused by the ball had lasted only an instant.

It had got dark, and we lost our way going back over the "Schmelz," and found ourselves crossing plowed fields. Beethoven hummed melodies to himself as he stumbled from one clod to another, awkwardly enough, and was glad to get help now and then, because of his shortsightedness. Upon arriving at the Rothes Haus, we separated. However my teacher went to his house with him and was invited afterwards to have some soup and eggs. There Beethoven spoke at length, as he had during the day, about his nephew Karl, who, a few days previously, had taken the desperate step of trying to shoot himself. One of the things he said was, "My Karl was in a boarding school; all they turn out is hothouse plants."

Once (perhaps in early spring of 1826) Beethoven and my father were talking about music as they so often did, and Beethoven asked my father whether he went to concerts. My father answered that he could not spare the time. "But what about Gerhard? Does Trouserbutton go? I'll send him tickets; I have them for the asking. Even if he doesn't understand anything, he will be learning how to listen, and that will help him." In the next few days my father received subscription tickets from Beethoven for me to the *Concerts spirituels* (given in the Landhaussaal at that time), and along with them a little rectangle of cardboard (like a cloakroom check), with only "No. 6" on it. – Father did not understand this, looked at it dubiously, and took it to be something that had accidentally got into the envelope; he therefore disregarded it. When we were walking together a few days later in the main avenue of the Schönbrunn Garden, my father remembered the tickets he had received, thanked him for them and asked whether the No. 6 meant anything. "Why yes, that is the ticket for the sixth of Schuppanzigh's quartet performances, which ends the cycle. And the performance is going on right now. It's a pity to miss something like that! How could you fail to understand it? It's obvious, or at least you should have asked me about it," etc. He kept going on about it and seemed disturbed and almost suspicious, as if we had purposely committed the oversight because we wanted to go on this walk. It was only after my father and I had repeatedly assured him that we both regretted it extremely, that he calmed down and enjoined me to attend the following concerts diligently. I made good use of the tickets thereafter; he sent them to me regularly as long as he lived, and to this I owe my best and first, and lasting, impressions of great music, and also my being able to hear the two Czernys, Linke, Schuppanzigh, Holz, Lutz, and C. M. von Bocklet, the only one still living, while they were at their best; and I also got to know Schubert, Weigl, Eybler, and other famous musical personalities among the audience.[134] I still remember vividly how Weigl and Eybler, and even Schindler, at the performance of the choral movement of the Ninth Symphony, shook their heads regretfully and expressed the opinion that here "Beethoven had gone too far after all."*[135] Not to speak of the Abbé Stadler and many other music lovers, who even in the 1840s, and even with Nicolai's unsurpassed performances, would stay for Mozart, Haydn, etc., but leave the hall when Beethoven's compositions began. —[137] How hard it can be for composers, once they have found their own path, to work their way up to complete awareness of such gigantic new creations was brought home to me by a statement made as late as 1863 by Schindler, who, after all, had frequently had the opportunity to go deeply into Beethoven's works. I asked him what he thought of the Mass in D. He replied: "A masterpiece, the greatest work of genius that ever was written, etc.; only it is too bad that Beethoven didn't cancel the trumpet entry in the Agnus Dei; it doesn't fit and has a disturbing effect." When I asked him, seeming to agree, whether he had talked to Beethoven about leaving the passage out, he answered: "Well, you know, nobody could ever say anything to him about his compositions; in fact, until a work was finished, he obstinately refused to let anybody even look at it, including me." – And yet how great and sublime this wonderful passage is!

Just as Beethoven had begun to be concerned about my musical taste, he had done the same from the outset with his nephew Karl. As Schindler said to me,† Karl must have had a high degree of musical sensitivity, and Beethoven would sometimes sing or play him a theme he had thought of for a projected work, in order to get his opinion and preference. But things did not progress well with his studies; his insuperable love for café life and running into debt was too strong for him. His loving uncle's most urgent warnings and most moving letters were of no avail, especially since every threat was annulled by assurances of the tenderest love and since Karl was constantly

---

* As many readers may know, Richard Wagner still encountered this kind of prejudice as to the Ninth Symphony in Dresden in 1846, and had to stand up for it, and felt compelled, in order to create some sort of understanding, to send out in advance an explanatory "program." (See Richard Wagner's *Gesammelte Schriften*, Vol. 11).[136]

† See also Schindler, 11, p. 7; Schindler–MacArdle, p. 234.

under the evil influence of his mother, an irredeemably dissipated woman, vulgar in feeling and in action.

The time came for the tests in engineering, and there were debts that had to be paid. Time was getting short and Karl, who knew that he was unprepared either in knowledge or in purse, and was more and more afraid of his uncle's reproaches, which "had been wearisome to him for a long time and which he found distasteful," resolved to alter his way of life, not for the better, as his uncle desired, but by killing himself. He bought two pistols, went to Baden, climbed the tower of the Rauhenstein ruins, put the two pistols to his temples and pulled the triggers, and wounded himself only superficially on the periosteum, but still seriously enough to have to be taken to Vienna to the General Hospital.

The news was shattering to Beethoven. The pain he felt at this event was indescribable; he was crushed, like a father who has lost his beloved son. My mother bumped into him on the Glacis; he was completely unnerved, "Do you know what has happened to me? My Karl shot himself!" – "And – is he dead?" "No, he only grazed himself, he is still alive, there is hope that he can be saved; – but the disgrace that he has caused me; I loved him so much!"

Ignaz Seng, the surgeon, who is still alive, told me the following story of his meeting with Beethoven: "I was an assistant at the Vienna General Hospital in the surgical division of Chief Physician Gassner, to which a part of what was known as the Three-Gulden floor also belonged; I lived to the left in the large court opposite the central building, where the office was, on the ground floor. Late in the summer of 1826, while I was doing my rounds, a man in a gray coat came up to me; on first sight I took him for a plain citizen. He asked dryly: 'Are you Assistant Dr. Seng? The office referred me to you. Is my scoundrel of a nephew in your ward?' I asked the name of the person being inquired after, answered the question in the affirmative and told him that the patient was in a room in the Three-Gulden floor, had had a gunshot wound dressed, and did he want to see him? Thereupon he said: 'I am Beethoven.' And as I was taking him up, he went on: 'Actually, I didn't want to see him; he doesn't deserve it, he has caused me too much trouble, but ...' and then he continued talking about the catastrophe and the change in his nephew's life and how he had spoiled him with too much kindness, etc. But I was completely astonished to see beneath this plain exterior the great Beethoven before me, and I promised him to take the best possible care of his nephew."

On one side the shot had missed completely; the superficial wound on the

PLATE 24   Karl van Beethoven.
Unsigned miniature portrait

other temple left only a small scar after healing, and Karl was able to cover it by combing his hair forward.

His uncle, much more deeply wounded, consulted at once with my father as to what would be the best thing to do with his unfortunate nephew. After long deliberation the two friends agreed to ask him whether he was willing to enter the army. After he had said he was, my father immediately took care of the necessary steps. Beethoven consented to meet all the expenses involved for kitting out the *ex propriis* cadet, "I only hope he will be a man worth something in his new condition." Since my father was a court councillor attached to the Court War Council, Lieutenant Field Marshal Baron Stutterheim[138] was kind enough to further the matter and take Karl into his regiment as an *ex propriis* cadet; he also assured my father that if Karl shaped up well, he would keep a place open for him as an officer in due course.

Beethoven gradually came to accept this prospect, still hoping that Karl would reform, although it hurt him deeply to have to give up the plans he had previously drawn up for his beloved nephew. But other sorrows were added to those already felt, even though Beethoven's noble soul was already tortured beyond endurance. The police entered the picture. They managed to arrive at the conclusion that the source of the trouble must have been insufficient religious instruction, which Karl was to receive at once from the police, since his paternal guardian "had proved so little able to give him adequate moral principles."[139] Beethoven's letters to Karl, which positively overflowed with moral preaching, really made any such imputations seem improbable! Once, in answer to an official inquiry as to proofs of his nobility, he had bluntly told them that his head and his heart were the seat of his nobility;[140] this suggestion from the police, coming on top of everything that had gone before, hit him so hard and so deeply that his health began to be shaken. –

My father and Schindler advised Beethoven to go on a vacation, and brother Johann, unfortunately, invited him to his estate in Gneixendorf near Krems. Ludwig, always ready to trust his brother, made the mistake of accepting the invitation. He had hardly arrived there when, in a few days, letters came to my father showing once more how the trustful Ludwig had fallen into the trap of his contemptible, greedy, miserly, heartless, and conscienceless brother; and my father began to be seriously concerned for Ludwig's health. Beethoven had been badly taken in. He had hoped, as he had been promised, to be able to continue his recovery for some time free from all cares, but when he had arrived at Johann's place, his brother had given him a bad room, in no way suitable for the cold wet November weather, with meager heating and sometimes none at all, bad food and not enough of it; and after three days, notice was given him that he would have to pay for his room and board;* Ludwig complained bitterly about this in a letter to my father from Gneixendorf;[142] and he had expected loving brotherly treatment! Then too there was the unpleasant company of Johann's wife and foster-daughter.[143] And yet, under domestic and social circumstances of this kind, detrimental to mind and body alike, his spirit was not at all broken. One more composition, his last one, his swan song, was created there in Gneixendorf, a fresh and imaginative work, overflowing with gay inspiration.

This was the finale to the Quartet in B-flat major, Op. 130† (instead of the well-known original fourth movement, the fugue for strings published separately by Artaria as Opus 133)[146] (Schindler, II, p. 115; Schindler–MacArdle, p. 308; and Thayer's *Chronologisches Verzeichnis der Werke Ludwig van Beethovens* [Berlin, 1865], p. 156). This is proof enough that when he was composing, Beethoven was not influenced by his momentary social circumstances; that is, the well of his inspiration and the character of his compositions were not dependent on his mood of the moment, as officious commentators would like to make it appear. – Ferdinand Hiller expresses the same sort of opinion in his article entitled "On December 17, 1870," *Kölnische Zeitung*, saying: "People are especially interested these days in making the most detailed investigations of the daily life of great men. There is nothing against that, so long as no attempt is made to bring their spiritual works and deeds into too close connection with the circumstances of their lives (which would lead to gross errors) or so long as misguided enthusiasm does not seek to find the significance of their productions in the tiniest details of their conduct and behavior."

* In the Gneixendorf conversation books for Fall 1826 (now in the Royal Library in Berlin), an entry in Johann's handwriting states: "If you want to live with us, you can have everything for 40 gulden C. M. monthly, that makes 500 gulden C. M. for the whole year."[141]

† On the same sheets of music paper on which this quartet's fourth movement was written by Beethoven in Gneixendorf,[144] there were also (see Nottebohm, *Beethoveniana*, p. 81) sketches, written in pencil, for a movement of a quintet in E major, with a statement of the theme. Nottebohm also speaks of finding some ideas for a four-hand piano sonata sketched on the same sheets. – I remember very well that the publisher who had commissioned this composition, Diabelli, during his visits in the course of Beethoven's illness, and in my presence, repeatedly urged him to complete this four-hand sonata, but Beethoven always refused. As soon as Diabelli had left, Beethoven would always say to me: "Diabelli badly wants me to work on this sonata and thinks he can force me to; but as long as I am sick, I won't work at anything."[145]

But the wretched conditions in Gneixendorf had a most adverse effect on his body, already badly debilitated by the trials it had undergone and so all the more susceptible to damage from harmful external influences.

Beethoven finally wearied of the unseemly way he had been received and treated in Gneixendorf, and, feeling unwell, he wanted to return to Vienna. Johann refused to let him have his good covered carriage and, in order to spare it, gave him a bad open one, notwithstanding the wet cold December day.[147] The result of this miserable homeward journey arranged by his brother was peritonitis. If the spirit and the body were enfeebled by physical or mental mistreatment, a harmful influence from outside can be very dangerous. – It can be medically proved that Beethoven's disease was peritonitis and not pneumonia, as the biographies erroneously* state; the reasons are the following: firstly, only peritonitis, and not pneumonia, can produce dropsy; secondly, although there was a catarrhal irritation of the respiratory organs at the beginning of the illness, he did not cough throughout his illness, his voice remained strong and he had no pain in breathing except to the extent that later the excessive accumulations of liquid in the abdomen exerted an alarmingly constricting pressure upwards; and finally, during the three days of his struggle for life his lungs were so completely healthy and strong that there could be no question of a previous pneumonia.[149]

And so, Beethoven returned to Vienna a sick man. Because of his clumsiness in practical matters, my father was not informed immediately of his return, although a previous letter from Ludwig had made my father deeply concerned over Beethoven's health.[150] Upon receiving it he had said, "I am afraid that Beethoven is dangerously ill, even dropsical." The content of the letter, which I was unable to find in the papers my father left, must have hinted at symptoms of some such disease; my father, although not a physician, was much in the company of doctors and recognized the danger. Meanwhile, the nephew, in his usual irresponsible way, must have reacted to his uncle's request to get him a doctor, first by forgetting it and then, a few days later, happening to remember it, while playing billiards at the cafe, and asking the marker to send a doctor to his uncle.[151] That is how Dr. Wawruch eventually called on the patient, who had become seriously ill in the meantime, and became Beethoven's official physician.

* Schindler says, (Schindler, II, p. 134; Schindler–MacArdle, p. 320) and the later biographers have taken it from him: "The disease of which Beethoven was a victim began as a pneumonia developing out of a chill in the abdomen," and he adds, "This was realized far too late by Dr. Wawruch and by the time the correct diagnosis had been made, the stage of dropsy had already been reached."[148]

PLATE 25   Dr. Andreas Ignaz Wawruch. Lithograph by Ziegler

Admittedly this man was professor at the medical clinic for surgeons, and was at that time a skilled and renowned practitioner of his specialty; he was also known as a good Latinist; but he had not proved himself to be a great physician. At the very least, what he prescribed in this case is shown to be simply unable to have attacked the disease at its root and have had a beneficial result.*

As soon as my father received news of Beethoven's arrival, he hurried over there, of course, and I along with him. Thereafter, being overloaded with official business, he could only get to his friend's bedside at about four o'clock and I stayed there every day before or after my lessons; my shift was from noon to 2.00 p.m. and from 3.00 p.m. to 4.00 p.m. or 5.00 p.m.

Excellent as the earlier times had been, the memory of them untroubled and unforgettable, there now began for me a more frequent and longer association, several hours every day, with the great man who was so dear to me; but it was a time of sadness, whose harsh impressions were ineradicably imprinted on my youthful mind.

During his sickness Beethoven lay, as he had when healthy, in the room with two windows (the one before one reached his study). The bed was against the wall that faced the ante-chamber door and separated the large room from the study where he composed. The head of the bedstead was

---

* A "Medical Survey of L. v. Beethoven's Last Period of Life," written by Dr. Andreas Wawruch immediately after the death of the great composer, was found among the physician's effects and published by Aloys Fuchs in the *Wiener Zeitschrift für Kunst, Literatur und Mode*, edited by Friedrich Witthauer (No. 86, April 30, 1842);[152] but it is teeming with errors and "bald statements dictated by vanity or other motives," and Anton Schindler, in the *Frankfurter Conversationsblatt*, edited by J. N. Schuster (No. 193, July 4, 1842), provided impartial and faithful corrections and responses, with references to his biography: "Regarding the events at Beethoven's bedside, virtually every medical visit and in general everything that happened there for four months took place either in my (Schindler's) presence or that of Imperial Court Councillor von Breuning or his son (the latter now a Doctor of Medicine), as the three of us took turns in this sacred duty," etc. It should also be mentioned that for the last eight years of Beethoven's life almost all the actions and conversations of that sad period are preserved in the master's conversation books (at that time in Schindler's possession, now in the Royal Library in Berlin), for the systematic utilization of which Schindler once hoped to find the right man, since he did not feel justified in doing it himself, as he appeared so often in the notebooks.

Dr. F. G. Wegeler, too (Wegeler–Ries, Supplement, p. 13; Eng. Edn., p. 154), confirms Schindler's suspicions of Dr. Waurauch (as he says, instead of the correct form Wawruch): "Dr. Malfatti had ordered iced punch for the dropsy patient, since as a friend of Beethoven's for many years he understood the latter's strong inclination for alcoholic drinks." Dr. Wegeler declares Wawruch's statement to be "completely unjustified."[153] – I can only attest that Wawruch's assertions came from someone who was no friend of Beethoven's at all, let alone a friend of many years' standing, and are so completely fanciful as to show they were written as apologetics.

against the back wall, so that Beethoven faced the two windows and his left side was towards the middle of the room; in this way he had a clear view of all of it.

To the left of the head of the bedstead was a bedside table and further along, towards the stove, a long table. Next to the bed was a small table with two or three chairs for the few friends who came to visit him. On the bedside table stood a black japanned box in which he kept his cash; on the floor alongside the bedside table, a little yellow folding writing desk.[154]

On the small table by the bed was an old door bell which Beethoven had brought with him when he had moved. It was primitive and anything but elegant but it gave good service now on account of its loud tone; for Sali the housekeeper could hear it through the walls even when she was far off in the back room. In addition, this table always had on it a conversation book made by folding and stitching a large sheet of writing paper into octavo format, along with a pencil for conversing with the deaf invalid, and a slate and slate pencil for the same purpose. Visitors wrote what they had to say on one or the other. I usually used the latter, and regret it now, for my part, since there are only rare records of my boyish conversations in entries made when I occasionally employed the notebook. But the essence of what I said at the time and the circumstances of the conversations are so deeply imprinted on my memory that I still remember most of it very well.

Fortunately, Schindler gathered up these conversation books, like so many other things, at Beethoven's death, and most of them are now in the Royal Library in Berlin. Had it not been for him, these notebooks, with all their copious materials on Beethoven's view on art and science and in particular the circumstances of his daily life, would have been scattered over the whole world, and most likely lost; and especially so since my father, excessively careful about what did not belong to him, would not take anything nor let me appropriate anything.

Although forty-seven years have passed since this mournful and unforgettable time at our great-hearted friend's bed of suffering it is hard for me to put the details down on paper without being overcome with emotion. I say "great-hearted," because it was very seldom that a sound of complaint came from his pain-stricken lips. Although he was no longer busy composing, he occupied himself with ideas for and about such things, with plans for creations that had long been on his mind (especially the Tenth Symphony), with events of the day that interested him, very much with the course of his illness, with his financial needs, which, because of the prospect

PLATE 26   Dr. Johann Seibert. Lithograph by Josef Kriehuber

of a long-drawn-out sickness and recuperation period, had begun to worry him, etc.

One noteworthy fact is that, at last, the problem of his nephew, which previously had tortured him so, seemed to have been solved for him, or at least eased, after my father had got the young man into a regiment, at Iglau. His feeling of gratitude towards the commander of the regiment, Lieutenant Field Marshal von Stutterheim, for his helpfulness towards my father and himself, led him to dedicate his String Quartet in C-sharp minor, Op. 131, to the Field Marshal.[155] On the other hand, he was angered daily by the useless visits of Professor Wawruch, who was soon making poor Beethoven drink a really astounding set of concoctions. Sali the housekeeper had already taken 80 six-ounce bottles back to the dispensary to get the two-kreutzer refund and it was not long before she had another eighty to collect the refund on. In addition, Wawruch had ordered him always to drink his water with a couple of teaspoons of cream of tartar and sugar added, and the quantities that I myself stirred in during the couple of hours of my daily visits added up to an unbelievable amount. It was all in vain; even a layman could see that such a procedure could not lead to any rational end; for treating the organism symptomatically is useless by itself unless it is coupled with action against the essence and basic cause of the illness. Fluid accumulated in the poor man's abdomen so that a puncture had to be performed on December 18, by Chief Surgeon Seybert.[156] Things had come to that pass because Wawruch had done nothing to rectify the underlying cause, and since nothing was done thereafter in that direction, the abdomen began at once to fill up again with fluid, even though for days after the operation an indeterminate amount of water oozed out through the incision, which repeatedly became inflamed.

Beethoven had also sent for his previous physicians, Professor Braunhofer (this alternative would have been no improvement) and Dr. Staudenheim, but both of them must have found that the distance was too great to the Schwarzspanierhaus, right on the Glacis, near the inner city, or at least this was their pretext, probably in fear that their fees would not be adequate.[157] Wawruch too seemed to have fears of the same kind, and occasionally told my father, Schindler, and others in my presence that the honorarium should always be kept in mind in the practice of medicine; in general his attitude was dry, almost indifferent, quite in contrast to what he said in the above-mentioned "Medical Survey;"[158] the result was that the futility of the therapy must have convinced Beethoven that this was not the doctor for him. My father also was not at all pleased with Wawruch's behavior; instead of helping the languishing patient, he used the presence of visitors to show off his Latin, which he spoke very well. It often happened, and gradually became the rule, that when Beethoven was conversing with me and I announced that Wawruch was coming through the adjoining room, he would turn to the wall saying, "Oh, that ass!" and then answer him only laconically, and finally he answered Wawruch's questions not at all. Wawruch's indifference and mercenary attitude, and even more so, the fact that, although Beethoven showed his lack of confidence in him more and more openly, he continued his visits with pedantic unconcern: even I was struck by all this, and since the patient's condition did not improve in any way, I became very uneasy. Wawruch's appearance on the scene made a most disagreeable impression on me. When I said as much to Beethoven after the doctor had left on one occasion, the master, who felt that he was getting sicker and sicker, broke out in violent tirades against him and almost as much so against Dr. Seybert, although he did say the latter was "better." But actually Seybert did not go any more deeply into the illness than was required for his interest in operation technique.

I wished I could have persuaded my father to do something about changing doctors, and hinted at it more than once; but my father could not intervene in the matter because of the strained state of his relations with Johann van Beethoven, and for other reasons.

Beethoven had another physician friend, a man who at that time was the most prominent medical man in Vienna. This was Dr. Malfatti. Beethoven sent for him; but the doctor who was highly regarded by the public felt that Beethoven had once insulted him, and refused to come. Further entreaties were required (see Schindler, II, p. 135; Schindler–MacArdle, p. 320) to bring this old friend to the bedside of the dying man.[159] I was present at the first visit and the few that followed it. Beethoven waited for him with the greatest eagerness and his face lighted up with delight as Malfatti entered. He seemed to be drawing long-dormant recuperative power from Malfatti's demeanor. But the physician, otherwise so intelligent, seems to have lacked inspiration in Beethoven's case. The iced punch ordered at the first visit "to raise the tone of the digestive apparatus, overweakened by Wawruch's excessive prescription of drugs,"[160] produced the desired stimulation but it disappeared all too soon. At a follow-up visit, only a few days after a second puncture had been made, he ordered a sort of steam bath which made the condition of the anxiously hopeful patient so much worse that it had to be dropped immediately, after only one application. – Jugs filled with hot water

PLATE 27   Dr. Johann Malfatti. Lithograph by Josef Kriehuber

were lined up in a bathtub; birch leaves were spread thickly and the patient was set down on them, while the bathtub and the body, except for the head, were covered with a sheet. Malfatti's intention was to stimulate the skin and get his system to produce a beneficial sweat, but it had the exact opposite of the intended effect. The body, which had been relieved of its fluid by the just-completed tapping operation, soaked up the liberated steam like a block of salt and swelled visibly while still in the contrivance, so that after a few days the drain had to be reintroduced in the still unhealed wound.

Beethoven awaited Malfatti's visits as eagerly as the coming of the Messiah, but he came only at intervals of several days, sending his assistant Dr. Röhrig, in the meantime, and even the visit of this substitute relaxed Beethoven's features and gave them a more cheerful aspect, despite his visible disappointment at not seeing the supposedly genuine savior in person. But once, when Malfatti failed altogether to come as he had promised, and Wawruch entered instead, I remember very clearly how Beethoven turned his body violently towards the wall and the word "ass" came from his mouth with unusual clarity, without Wawruch's hearing it, or at least without his showing any signs of having done so.

When brother Johann came in, I frequently heard the disappointed exclamation, "Oh, it's him again," but when Schindler entered, or my father, or even I, insignificant boy as I was, he always greeted us with a friendly smile.

But I will give myself and my readers respite from the dreary picture of illness and change the subject to some other events that took place during that painful period.

Here I must mention that my wish to be close to Beethoven every day had been so completely fulfilled, and my next cherished wish was to use the familiar "Du" with him, as my father did. I had been devoted to him for a long time and was proud that he liked me, making me one of a very few of the elect in that respect. I asked my father how I might lead up to it, whether he would act as my agent, or whether I should ask for permission myself. Unhesitatingly, my father answered: "If that gives you pleasure, you don't need all these ceremonies; just address him in that way; he won't mind at all, in fact he'll rather be glad of it, if he notices it at all." On the basis of this consent, and knowing how well my father knew Beethoven's way of thinking, I ventured it at my next visit, when I was alone with Beethoven (this was in the first stages of his illness), with beating heart but boldly, and wrote down my first words in the conversation books using this form of address. I looked at his face intently as I held the slate up in front of him. – It turned out as my father had predicted; Beethoven did not notice it at all, and that was that.

And now for some of the events.

During his illness, towards mid-February 1827, Handel's collected works were delivered one morning, bound, in a fine quarto edition, sent as a gift by Stumpff, the harp virtuoso.[161] He had long wished to have it and the gift was made in response to his longstanding wish, which was voiced only once. When I came into his room at noon, as I did every day, he pointed, with his eyes beaming, at the volumes piled up on one of the two pianos: "See, I received these as a gift today; they have given me great joy with this. I have wanted them for a long time; for Handel is the greatest, the ablest composer; I can still learn from him. Bring the books over to me." He kept on saying these and similar things, in happy excitement. And now I began to bring one volume after another over to his bed. He leafed through one volume after another as I gave them to him, sometimes stopping at particular passages, and then put one volume after another to his right on his bed up against the wall, finally making a heap that remained there for hours, because I found them still piled up when I came again in the afternoon. And again he started to sing the praises of the great Handel and to call him the most classic and most accomplished of all composers.[162]

Once, when I arrived, I found him sleeping, as often happened. I sat down at his bedside and kept still in order not to wake him from his sleep, which it was hoped would give him strength. Meanwhile, I leafed through and read in the conversation books that were still on the bedside table to be used, to see who had been there in the meantime and what they had talked about. One thing I found there was: "The quartet of yours that Schuppanzigh played yesterday didn't go over very well."[163] When he woke up a little later, I held that bit up in front of him, asking what he had to say about that. "It will please them some day" was the laconic answer he gave me; and to that he added, fully and firmly aware that he wrote as he thought fit, and was not led astray by the judgments of his contemporaries: "I know; I am an artist."*

---

* Schindler (II, p. 281; Schindler–MacArdle, pp. 444–5) answers the question often put him by music lovers, "whether Beethoven ever expressed the hope that his works would some day receive the appreciation they deserved," with "Never." he added a quiet conjecture: "He may have hoped that at some distant future time all his works might be revived; except for the symphonies and quartets, he had seen all his other works die." For example, Schindler adds, Beethoven underscored and copied into his diary the following words from Goethe's *West-östlichen Divan*, where, in the introduction, Goethe speaks of the understanding for his more difficult works that would come, sooner or only after years: "... and a second, a third generation coming into being will reward me doubly and triply for the tribulations I had to endure

Since we were alone, we got to talking about musical works, and I took the opportunity to ask why he had not written a second opera, although my father had told me, long before this, that one main reason was the many sorrows and difficulties he had had with the staging of *Fidelio*, as well as the fact that this opera had been so little appreciated and had earned him so little money. He replied, "I wanted to write one more opera, but I haven't found a suitable libretto for it. I need something that inspires me; it has to be something moral, edifying. I would never havé been able to set to music texts like those Mozart composed. I could never get into the mood with a disreputable libretto. I have been given many suggested librettos but, as I said, nothing I could care for." (See above.) Then he added: "There is much that I still want to write. Right now, the Tenth Symphony,* and I would like to compose a Requiem, and the music for *Faust*; yes, and a piano method too. This I would do entirely differently from the way the others have done it. Now I won't get around to all that any more, and in general, I don't work when I'm sick, no matter how much pressure Diabelli and Haslinger put on me. I have to be in the right state for it. Many times I haven't been able to compose for long periods of time; but it always comes back sooner or later."[166]

At another time, I found a music notebook on a piece of furniture in the room. It was completely full of notes, written in fits and starts, and even additional staves drawn freehand right across the margins, with all kinds of musical thoughts entered on them; it was a remarkable sight.†[167] I held it up to him, and asked whether he really needed to make notes of his inspirations; for at that time it still seemed implausible to me that such a great mind needed such aids to his memory, just as less gifted people do. Beethoven answered: "I always have a notebook like that with me (it was rather heavy machine-made writing paper, cross-lined, simply folded and fastened), and

from my earlier contemporaries." Further, in a conversation with friends about the floods of Italian music, Beethoven had said emphatically: "Well, they can't take away from me my place in the history of music."[164] The answer he gave me, "It will please them one day," is further reason for hoping that Beethoven, however misunderstood and mistreated by most of his contemporaries, still derived some consolation from his awareness of his own artistry, although from hope to enjoyment there is a great gap.

* At that time, when in his last days he had received a gift of a hundred pounds sent on March 1, 1827 by the London Philharmonic Society, he intended to dedicate the Tenth Symphony to that society.[165] I have the impression that Beethoven had it in mind to employ English folk airs in that work; but Schindler contradicted that vague idea of mine.

† Aloys Fuchs later had two notebooks of this kind in Vienna. He told me once, when he showed them to the young Mendelssohn, the youth immediately recognized where Beethoven had used each of the ideas, and played them off on the piano. Fuchs was so amazed at his brilliancy that he presented one of the notebooks to the perceptive youth.[168]

PLATE 28   Rohrau. Birthplace of Josef and Michael Haydn

when an idea comes to me, I put it down at once. I even get up in the middle of the night when a thought comes, because otherwise I might forget it."

At another time (in mid-February) Diabelli brought Beethoven, as a gift, the lithograph he had just published of Haydn's poverty-stricken birthplace in the Moravian village of Rohrau.[169] The picture caused him great pleasure; when I came at noon, he showed it to me at once: "Look, I got this today. Just see the little house, and such a great man was born in it. Your father must have a frame made for me; I'm going to hang it up." In the afternoon, when I came back, this time with my father, Beethoven repeated his wish. I took the picture at once and my father asked my piano teacher to order a simple frame for it, of black polished wood, as Beethoven had requested, and then to bring the framed picture back as soon as possible. Heller was over-joyed at the honor of being able to do something for the great Beethoven and not only got the frame made in a couple of days, but had added in a fair round hand on the white margin at the bottom, "Jos. Hayden's Birthplace in Rohrau." I pointed out the error, Hayden instead of Haydn, to my father. He told me not to worry about the mistake, that Beethoven wouldn't notice it. This was the case, when I handed the picture over to Beethoven, but I was disobedient enough to call his attention to the error. The reaction to this foolish remark was typical. At once Beethoven lost his temper just as deeply as he had been pleased at first at seeing the handsomely framed picture. His face turned red with rage and he asked me angrily: "Who wrote that, anyway?" "My piano teacher." "What's that ass's name? An ignoramus like that calls himself a piano teacher, calls himself a musician, and can't even spell the name of a master like Haydn. He's got to correct that right away; it's an outrage," etc. I was sorry that I had put my good teacher in a false position with Beethoven, and tried in every way I could to cover up the mistake, and also said my father had forbidden me to mention it: "You wouldn't notice it." But he got all the angrier and he explained to me that it was only at first glance that he would have overlooked it but later he couldn't have missed it; nobody of any education would, etc. The upshot was that I took the picture back home and had to have the mistake erased, and got a scolding from my father for my gratuitous comment. When I brought the picture back in a couple of days, Beethoven grumbled again over the error, and all he would say to my repeated efforts to excuse my teacher was: "He may be all right as a teacher, but as a man he is superficial, and he, like the majority, has not learned anything more and doesn't try to learn anything more than the absolute minimum."

This simple little picture led to still another typical scene. At my father's next visit, Beethoven started again to express doubts about my piano teacher's ability in view of the spelling error he had made. My father reassured him about that, but then Beethoven asked how much he had paid for the frame. My father didn't want to mention the paltry sum, but Beethoven insisted. "All right, then," my father wrote, "two gulden fifteen kreuzer W. W." (which was just about what it must have been). Beethoven said, "Take the little black box on the bedside table; you'll find money in it." Father did that, but there was no suitable small change, and so he took out a five-gulden note to change. Beethoven, who was tired and sleepy, had closed his eyes in the meantime. When my father saw that, he waited there with the box open, until Beethoven opened his eyes again, so that he could show him what he had taken out and how much he had put back, after which, being pressed for time, he hurried out to his office. Beethoven had not paid any attention and merely, as if disturbed in his sleep, waved it off with a curt, "Fair enough." But my father had hardly got out of the door, thereby waking Beethoven up completely, before Beethoven said he was insulted over the mistrust his friend had shown, and said to me in an irritated tone, "Now why did your father show me the banknote? Does he think I have no confidence in his honesty? I think that we are old enough friends to be convinced of each other's honesty," and so on and so forth. This trivial incident shows how sensitive and easily hurt Beethoven's gentle nature was. It had offended him that his friend should have imputed such a base quality to him. But Stephan was just as easily wounded. One day, during Beethoven's illness, a letter came addressed to "Herr Ludwig van Beethoven, Tonsetzer in Wien." My father was seriously displeased that the writer had used the word *Tonsetzer* (composer) instead of *Tondichter* (tone-poet) "as if he were a potter, all they needed was to put an *h* in the word *Ton*."[170] The fact is that my father was often upset over his poor sick friend, because of the scant sympathy shown the great man during his suffering.

But how good-hearted Beethoven was, how he let a child like me prattle on for hours, how he humored all my infantile notions, is shown by the following episode. I had composed a waltz, an utterly trivial waltz, and put it down on paper, and desperately wanted to show it to Beethoven, to hear what he would say, how he would like it. In my timorous vanity, I asked my parents whether I could dare to show it without being laughed out of court. When the answer came back yes, I acted swiftly. I hurried over at noon, with my sheet of music paper in my pocket. Although he was almost always alone, just that day Tobias Haslinger and his son Karl were there. That made me unhappy; it made me still shyer. I waited, but in vain, for the two to leave. They stayed on, and it was getting close to my dinner hour, when I had to be home. My impatience increased, and although I could probably have had the chance to be alone with Beethoven that afternoon, and certainly the next day, my haste would not let me rest. I overcame my twofold timidity, first with respect to Beethoven, for all my daily dealings with him, and that day in the presence of the two musically sophisticated Haslingers. Taking advantage of a pause in the conversation, I pulled my music out of my pocket and wrote on the slate about daring to try my hand at composing, and handed both items, writing and music to Beethoven. "Well," he said smiling, "let's see what you've done." He took the sheet, read it over carefully, asked for a pencil and said: "There are no mistakes in it except this, that you have the same note in the bass as in the treble." He wrote in the right note and handed the manuscript back to me. Haslinger also had a chance to look at my creation. The offhand way in which he put it down soon gave me a good idea as to what my product was worth. Unfortunately, this composition was lost, together with the above-mentioned twelve letters from Beethoven to me, when we moved after my father's death.

The only people who visited Beethoven daily during his illness were my father, me, Schindler, brother Johann, and (so long as he was still in Vienna) nephew Karl. Karl Holz came frequently, Tobias Haslinger now and then, alone or with his son Karl; occasionally there were Diabelli, Baron Eskeles's major domo Rau, the well-known pianist and teacher Dolejalek, and the virtuoso violinist Clement.[171] Among the Vienna friends the singer Mme. Schechner (died 1870), and Hummel with his student, the fifteen-year-old Ferdinand Hiller.*[172] Apart from these there were at most a couple of others: Schindler's sister, and Baron Gleichenberg, as can be seen from the conversation books.[174]

Rau usually brought stewed fruit from the mistress of his house. Beethoven seldom touched it, and I got to eat most of it. This, some bottles of wine from Malfatti, the picture of Haydn's birthplace, Handel's works and lastly £100 from the London Philharmonic Society (with the encouraging letter, extending their readiness to serve his needs and desires in the future):[175] these were the tokens of friendship that the ailing Beethoven received. These few visits, however, were a source of great pleasure to him. Malfatti's visits electrified him, because he put all his hopes for recovery in Malfatti's skill. But Malfatti came all too seldom, and as a rule it was only the two other physicians, who proved to be helpless in the situation.

Helpless they were, for nothing they could do by way of medicine or surgery brought about the slightest improvement or even arrested the advance of the disease. In short, the tapping of the liquid, once begun, had to be repeated soon, and then at shorter and shorter intervals. Fluid collected again in the abdomen more and more rapidly; edematous swellings of the lower parts of the body took on alarming proportions; lying down became very painful; the wound from the operation was dangerously inflamed, and water trickled from it, in fact flowed from it, until it reached the middle of the room; the patient's strength ebbed, and the end drew near.

It was suggested to him that he should comply with the practices of the Catholic Church, and he submitted to this ceremony with stoic calm.[176] It was later said by some people† that after the priest had left Beethoven said, "Plaudite amici, finita est comedia" (Applaud, friends, the comedy is over). Schindler told me, when I visited him in Bockenheim, that Beethoven had said these words when the doctors had gone away on one occasion, after a

---

* Dr. Ferdinand Hiller has published his interesting and truthful memories of those days, "Aus den letzten Tagen Ludwig van Beethovens" in the *Kölnische Zeitung*, Dec. 16, 1870 (also reprinted separately).[173] It contains many details confirming what I have reported.

† G. Mensch also says this in his biography of Beethoven, p. 288.

long consultation, and that is definitely my memory of it too.[177]* I can say quite definitely that my father, Schindler, and I were present, and that he quoted these words in his favorite sarcastic, comic manner in order to convey the idea: nothing can be done; the doctors' work is finished, or my life is over. I feel called upon to stress this clear recollection of mine because I have had the experience of hearing the overly devout denounce Beethoven as a mocker of religion, when in fact he had an ideal faith in God, as is shown by his marginal notes, etc.[178]

Two days before the actual end, when Beethoven's strength began to decline visibly and there could be no doubt that death was near, my father went about a painful duty in the afternoon, the task of submitting some necessary papers to Ludwig to sign. My father had hesitated for a long time, and consulted with Schindler and Johann, as to whether this had to be done or could be put off for a little later, so that poor Beethoven would not realize that the time had come for him to wind up his affairs. But in the meantime his consciousness was repeatedly fading, which aroused fears that he might soon lose the power of thought entirely, while suggesting the hope that Beethoven might be less perturbed by the documents. The papers he had to sign had long since been discussed with him and he had agreed to their contents; what he wanted was known. He had to affix his signature to his last will and testament, to the transfer of the guardianship of his nephew Karl to my father, and then a third signature, if I am not mistaken, to a letter to Dr. Bach as administrator of the estate.†[179] Father, Schindler, and Johann told Beet-

---

* Anselm Hüttenbrenner (died in Graz, 1868) wrote to A. W. Thayer from Hallerschloss, Graz, on August 20, 1860:

> It is not true that I asked Beethoven to take the sacraments for the dying; it is true that, at the request of the wife of the late music publisher, Tobias Haslinger, I had Jenger and Frau van Beethoven, wife of the landowner, ask Beethoven, in the gentlest way possible, to strengthen himself by partaking of Holy Communion. It is a complete myth that Beethoven said to me "Plaudite amici, comoedia finita est"; I was not even present when the last rites for the dying were administered on the morning of March 24, 1827. Beethoven certainly did not say anything of the sort, so contrary to his respectable nature, to any one else either. Frau van Beethoven did tell me, on the day her brother-in-law died, that after he had received the sacrament he said to the priest: "Father! I thank you! You have brought me comfort!"

† To Dr. Bach, Vienna, Wednesday, January 3, 1827: Respected Friend!
  Before my death I declare that Karl van Beethoven, my beloved nephew, is the sole heir to all my property, including, chiefly, seven bank shares and whatever cash may remain on hand. – Should the laws prescribe alterations pertaining to this bequest, then try to turn them so far as possible to my nephew's *advantage* – I appoint you *his trustee* and ask you together with his guardian, Hofrat von Breuning, to be a father to him – May God preserve you – A thousand thanks for the love and friendship you have shown me –

hoven, already half asleep, that he would have to sign something, propped him up as best they could with pillows, and gave him the documents one after the other, with my father dipping the pen into the ink afresh each time and putting it into his hand.* The dying man, whose hand was otherwise so firm and bold, now painfully, with faltering hand, wrote his immortal name for the last time, still legibly but forgetting a letter in the middle of his name, in one instance the h, in another an e.[181] Schindler would have liked to get his very last signature on the manuscript score of the *Fidelio* overture, which Beethoven had recently presented to him,† but the effort of writing the other signatures had exhausted Beethoven so, and the moment was so moving, that out of emotion and pity he refrained from carrying out his wish.

Actually, the action could not have been carried out at any later juncture, for as soon as it was over, his delirium intensified with every sign of the death agony. This was at five in the afternoon, March 24, 1827, after we had left the room.

On the next day and the day after that the powerful man lay there unconscious, breathing with a very audible rattling noise. His strong body and unimpaired lungs (see p. 87) struggled titanically with approaching death. It was a terrible sight. And yet we knew that the poor man was no longer suffering; all the same, it was hideous to see this noble being so irrevocably disintegrating that all communication with him was impossible. On 25

Ludwig van Beethoven
To Herr v. Bach, Gentleman, Dr. of Laws, dwelling in the Wollzeille.[180]

* As my father did with Beethoven, it fell to my lot to get Grillparzer's last signature. On January 21, 1872, from half past seven to noon, I was with the writer, whose strength had suddenly failed in the last few days. Shortly before I left, Miss Josefa (Josefine) Fröhlich came into the room to suggest that he should sign the royalties statement for the last quarter, which the management of the Burgtheater had sent over. Grillparzer, who was reclining in his arm-chair, opened his eyes, read the paper through twice, and asked for the money. Since the man from the theater had it in the waiting room, Miss Fröhlich went to get it. Grillparzer tried, in vain, to sit up; I took a thick book (Voltaire, as I later saw) from his desk, put it on his right knee as a support for the paper to be signed, put one of the three pens on the desk into his hand, supported him in as comfortable a position as possible, and so he wrote his name, although his hand trembled badly, down to the z. Then the book and the receipt fell off his knee; I put them back quickly and he added the mising e and r, and his usual flourish. Then Miss Fröhlich came·in with the money. I asked for the pen as a memento, which the lady granted me, with her customary kindness. Two hours later, at about 1.45 p.m., while my colleague, Medical Councillor Dr. Preyss, was in the room, Grillparzer passed away in the same armchair. When I came back shortly after two, he was no longer alive. The pen that the "Green Island" Society received shortly after Grillparzer's death is one of the other two (all three were goose quills, with steel nibs attached) that I had left lying on the desk and that had remained there after the poet's death.

† Schindler, I, p. 129; Schindler–MacArdle, p. 129.

March it was not expected that he would survive the night; but on the twenty-sixth we found him still alive, breathing even louder than before. March 26, 1827 was the sad day of Beethoven's death.

My father, Schindler, brother Johann, and I were standing around the bed in the afternoon. We could already hear the hoarse breathing getting weaker and weaker. It would have been a blessing for him to die. Although there had been a good deal of snow that winter in February and March, it had melted a few days ago. This afternoon, however, mighty masses of clouds were piling up in the sky. My father and Schindler, badly depressed by the prolonged death process and talking about the various things that would have to be done immediately after Beethoven's death which would claim their painfully limited time, decided then and there to find a suitable site for the grave, and left the death chamber. Father's Julie was in the cemetery of the village of Währing (see p. 39); her parents were buried there too and we had often gone there together. It was a place of sadness that was less alien to us than other cemeteries. I immediately asked my father to find a resting place for Beethoven there as well. He took up this suggestion all the more willingly since he too was to be buried there one day. However, there was no room left near Julie's grave and the spot for himself, but there were some a few places above the "Resting Place of the Vering Family," and this unexpected circumstance brought the two friends a little closer together, even after death; for when my father's death followed not long after, he was buried, as his brother-in-law Vering requested, not next to Julie but in the Vering family vault.

I had stayed in the room of the dying man with Beethoven's brother Johann and Sali the housekeeper. It was between four and five o'clock; the dense clouds drifting together from every quarter increasingly obscured the daylight and, all of a sudden, a violent storm broke, with driving snow and hail. Just as in the immortal Fifth Symphony and the everlasting Ninth there are crashes that sound like a hammering on the portals of Fate, so the heavens seemed to be using their gigantic drums to signal the bitter blow they had just dealt the world of art. At about 5.15 I was called home to my teacher. The end could be expected any minute; I left him alive, or at least still breathing, for the last time.

I had hardly been home half an hour when the housekeeper came over to tell us that death had come at about 5.45. At the last moment, Anselm Hüttenbrenner of Graz happened to be there.[*]

* Anselm Hüttenbrenner writes (August 20, 1860) in the above-mentioned letter to A. W. Thayer: " ... When I entered Beethoven's bedroom about three o'clock in the afternoon

PLATE 29   Beethoven on his death-bed. Pencil drawing by Joseph Teltscher

Aloys Fuchs later, shortly before he died, showed me a water-color sketch with my father, Schindler, Johann, Hüttenbrenner and me standing around Beethoven's deathbed.[183] This would have to be corrected in keeping with what has been said above, but is otherwise accurate.

Everything we now have to say no longer relates to the living Beethoven among us, but only to the heritage of his genius, his immortal creations.

Tragoedia finita erat.

(The tragedy was finished.)

March 26, 1827, I found there Court Councillor von Breuning, his son, and Frau van Beethoven, the wife of Johann van Beethoven, landowner and apothecary in Graz, and also my friend, Josef Teltscher, portrait painter.

I believe that Prof. Schindler was there too. The gentlemen mentioned very soon left the room where the dying composer was wrestling with death and expressed their lack of hope of finding him still alive when they returned. At Beethoven's last moment there was no one in the room but Frau van Beethoven and I ...."[182]

On the next day the funeral notices appeared, composed by my father.*
Danhauser asked my father for permission to take a death mask, which was
granted.[184] My father's letter on that is given in facsimile in Schindler (II,
pp. 149–150; Schindler–MacArdle, pp. 330–331).

On this day the following scene (frequently told wrong) took place in the
study of Beethoven's apartment: my father had gone to the dwelling of the
deceased with Beethoven's brother Johann, Schindler, and Holz to look over
the papers that had been left, and in particular the seven bank shares that
were to go to the nephew as sole heir. It was known that they had to be somewhere, but no one knew where Beethoven kept them. My father was sure
they were in the (already mentioned) yellow writing desk alongside the
bedside table. They were not to be found there or anywhere else, and Johann
was already dropping hints that the search was only a pretense; my father
came home to dinner in a state of high excitement, and went back in the
afternoon at once to renew the search with those named above. From what
father said later, the scene became pretty tense, until Holz accidentally pulled
on a nail projecting from a cupboard; a drawer and with it the long sought
after papers dropped out.†

In the evening the autopsy was made by Dr. Johann Wagner, Rokitansky's
predecessor.[186] In a careful examination of the long-since devastated hearing
organs of the Titan of music, the petrous portion of the temporal bone was
sawn through and removed. (Court Councillor Hyrtl recently explained to
me, as he showed me Mozart's skull, proving its authenticity by complete
documentation,[187] that when he was a student, he had for a long time seen
those hearing organs preserved in a sealed glass vessel in the possession of the
veteran coroner Anton Dotter; later they disappeared.) Only when Beet-

---

* "Invitation to the funeral of Ludwig van Beethoven, which will take place March 29, at three
o'clock. The meeting place will be at the residence of the deceased, in Schwarzspanierhaus,
No. 200, on the Glacis facing the Schottenthor. From there the procession will go to the
Church of the Trinity of the Minorite Fathers in the Alsergasse.

"The musical world suffered the irreplaceable loss of the renowned composer on March 26,
1827, towards six in the evening. Beethoven died of dropsy in his fifty-sixth year, after receiving the holy sacraments. The day of interment will be communicated later by L. van Beethoven's admirers and friends.

"(This card is issued in Tob. Haslinger's Music Store).
                                "Printed by Anton Strauss."
(I owe the possession of an original of this notice to a recent gift from my friend, the conductor
M. Durst.)

† Accordingly, these securities, along with the letters to Countess Giulietta Guicciardi, were
not, as the *Grazer Tagespost* erroneously reported, found in the "secret drawer of the desk"
now in my possession.[185]

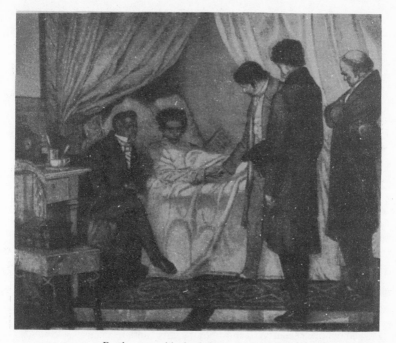

PLATE 30   Beethoven on his death-bed, with friends in attendance.
Unsigned water-color

hoven's body was lifted out of the bed for performing the autopsy, did we realize what terrible bed sores he had. Throughout his agony he had seldom uttered a word of complaint, and the conversation books have only a single place where my father promised to get a salve to heal a bed sore. He complained more to me, and more often, about the pain he felt at the inflamed operation wound.

On March 28 Beethoven's body lay in state in the two-windowed room in front of the door to the study, his face turned towards the entrance door. Because the temporal bone had been excised, the joint of the lower jaw had no support (the glenoid cavity being missing) and as a result the face was badly distorted, and bore little resemblance to the face in life (see Danhauser's very accurate lithographic portrait dated March 28).

On March 29 I went with my father to Beethoven's dwelling and wanted to cut off a lock of his hair. Father had not allowed me to do this before the lying-in-state ended, in order not to spoil his appearance; but now we found that strangers had already cut off all his hair.*

The funeral procession took place at three in the afternoon. During Beethoven's long illness the Viennese had seemed virtually to have forgotten him; the news of his death had shaken people out of their apathy. Several hours before the appointed time a vast throng had assembled before the Schwarzspanierhaus, and columns of participants and the merely curious converged constantly from all directions. As many as 20,000 people filled the space from the house to the part of the Glacis where the Votivkirche now stands. All the well-known figures of the art world had turned up. The singers of the excellent Italian opera company then resident in Vienna (under Barbaja's management) had expressed their desire to sing during the ceremony.[188] The crowds kept getting thicker and thicker. When the coffin was taken down the stairs and set down in the court behind the main gate, and the Italian singers around it tried to sing in mourning, people began to rush into the house in such swarms that nothing could have been heard. My father had thought in advance that such crowds might be present and had asked the Alser barracks nearby to send some troops; the gate to the house was now barred. When the coffin was taken up after the singing and the gate was opened, the crowd pushed out of the courtyard and from the street and up against the coffin, so much so that we four pallbearers: Beethoven's brother Johann, my father, Schindler, and I, instead of being right behind the coffin, only got back into the procession, and well to the rear at that, after the coffin had already reached the corner of the Rothes Haus. Eight Kapellmeister: Eibler, Hummel, Seyfried, Kreutzer, Weigl, Gyrowetz, Würfel, and Gänsbacher, held the ends of the shroud.†[189] A large number of musicians, holding candles, surrounded the coffin.

The procession seemed endless; the restless throngs of people numbered

---

* When Schubert's remains were exhumed on October 13, 1863, we found his hair all there, in great abundance, with a wreath of flowers around it and a part of a comb holding it together.
† Ferdinand Hiller says, very rightly, in his Memorial and in the *Kölnische Zeitung* (December 1871): "The coffin was covered with wreaths – there were no medals on it – Beethoven never received any."

   I was told on one occasion that when Beethoven was asked whether he wanted a decoration or money from King Friedrich Wilhelm III for dedicating the Ninth Symphony to him, he is supposed to have answered promptly, "Money." How much truth there is in this I have no way of knowing; but Beethoven wrote to Wegeler on October 7, 1826: "I have heard some talk of the Order of the Red Eagle, Second Class; I don't know what will come of that; I have never sought for such honors, but as things go in these days, it would not be unwelcome, for various reasons" (Wegeler–Ries, p. 50; Eng. edn., p. 49).[190] He received a ring with a couple of stones of no great value.

some thousands; all Vienna seemed to be on the move. Beethoven's Funeral March (from the Piano Sonata, Op. 26) was played as the coffin rounded the corner of the Rothes Haus, and the procession moved on to the parish church in the Alserstrasse. On the steps of the church there was such a crush, as bad as at the Schwarzspanierhaus, that the military guard now held us back, and it was only with great difficulty, after we had pointed to the crape bands on our hats, that we finally got into the already overcrowded church.

There the solemn blessing was given, and the procession moved on to Währing Cemetery, where the funeral oration composed by Beethoven's friend Grillparzer was to have been delivered. Since at that time it was forbidden to make such speeches on consecrated ground, Heinrich Anschütz delivered the moving address in solemn tones over the coffin in front of the cemetery gate.[191] Many tears were shed, here and at the grave, as the mighty Titan was lowered into the narrow grave and his friends and admirers cast the first earth over his remains.

There was a good deal of talk at that time to the effect that a reward had been offered for Beethoven's skull, and the rumor had spread so persistently that my father had discussed with Johann, Schindler, and Holz the advisability of lowering the coffin in reversed position, i.e., with the feet towards the outer wall. The idea was that, although watchmen had been engaged for the first few nights, there was a good chance they might doze off and it would be possible to tunnel under the wall and reach the head. Finally, the idea was dropped.

Grillparzer's words delivered by Anschütz at the grave of Beethoven, were the following, as Grillparzer transmitted them to my father at his personal request, and as I copied them then and there:[192]

Standing by the grave of him who has passed away, we are in a manner the representatives of an entire nation, of the whole German people, mourning the loss of the one highly acclaimed half of that which was left us of the departed splendor of our native art, of the fatherland's full spiritual bloom. There yet lives – and may his life be long! – the hero of verse in German speech and tongue; but the last master of tuneful song, the organ of soulful concord, the heir and amplifier of Händel and Bach's, of Haydn and Mozart's immortal fame is now no more, and we stand weeping over the riven strings of the harp that is hushed.

The harp that is hushed! Let me call him so! For he was an artist, and all that was his, was his through art alone. The thorns of life had wounded him deeply, and as the castaway clings to the shore, so did he seek refuge in thine arms, O thou glorious sister and peer of the Good and the True, thou balm of wounded hearts, heaven-born

Art! To thee he clung fast, and even when the portal was closed wherethrough thou hadst entered in and spoken to him, when his deaf ear had blinded his vision for thy features, still did he ever carry thine image within his heart, and when he died it still reposed on his breast.

He was an artist – and who shall arise to stand beside him?

As the rushing behemoth spurns the waves, so did he rove to the uttermost bounds of his art. From the cooing of doves to the rolling of thunder, from the craftiest inter-weaving of well-weighed expedients of art up to that awful pitch where planful design disappears in the lawless whirl of contending natural forces, he had traversed and grasped it all. He who comes after him will not continue him; he must begin anew, for he who went before left off only where art leaves off. Adelaide – and Leonora! Triumph of the heroes of Vittoria – and the humble[1] sacrificial song of the Mass! – Ye children of the twice and thrice divided voices! heaven-soaring harmony: "Freude, schöner Götterfunken," thou swansong! Muse of song[2] and the seven-stringed lyre! Approach his grave and bestrew it with laurel!

He was an artist, but a man as well. A man in every sense – in the highest. Because he withdrew from the world, they called him a man-hater, and because he held aloof from sentimentality, unfeeling.[3] Ah, one who knows himself hard of heart, does not shrink! The finest[4] points are those most easily blunted and bent or broken! An excess of sensitiveness avoids a show of feeling! He fled the world because, in the whole range of his loving nature, he found no weapon[5] to oppose it. He withdrew from mankind after he had given them his all and received nothing in return.[6] He dwelt alone, because he found no second Self. But to the end his heart beat warm for all men, in fatherly affection for his kindred, for the world his all and his heart's blood.

Thus he was, thus he died, thus he will live to the end of time.

You, however, who have followed[7] after us hitherward, let not your hearts be troubled![8] You have not lost him, you have won him. No living man enters the halls of the immortals. Not until the body has perished, do their portals unclose. He whom you mourn stands from now onward among the great of all ages, inviolate forever. Return homeward therefore, in sorrow, yet resigned! And should you ever in times to come feel the overpowering might of his creations like an onrushing storm, when your mounting ecstasy overflows in the midst of a generation yet unborn, then remember this hour, and think, We were there, when they buried him, and when he died, we wept.

Of other poetic tributes published and distributed at the graveside on that great day of sorrow I introduce the following:

BEETHOVEN

A poem by Gabriel Seidl[193]

You heard him yourselves! The sound of the message he addressed to you has only
    just faded away. You heard him yourselves! With a thousand tongues he
    summoned up for you the angels of emotion.
You heard him yourselves! Heard him! *Saw* him. For whoever heard him can also

picture in his soul the noble master's image. No painter portrays him as he portrays himself.

As his palette, he paints in sounds; for the canvas on which he paints, the human soul. On it he imprints with his brush the songs of his whole being, his image, in pleasure and in pain.

Listen to the mighty floods of his solemn power and you will catch a vision of the man himself, so charged with power and high purpose. Listen to his song, feel it: he would shame the sweet passion of a youthful soul.

Listen to the mighty roar of his battle thunder and you will catch a vision of his spirit, ready for the fray. Listen to the psalms of his choruses of supplication and you will see a heart that orbits God's throne.

Now he seizes sounds as the innocent soul seizes butterflies and then releases them; he wrestles with himself in ever-fluctuating combat and dissolves in tender longing at the end.

Now he plunges into life's cosmic ocean and reflects its struggles and its calm. Now he mocks himself, then us, then himself again; and skips in play to capture weighty eternal truths.

Deaf to the barren tumult of the outer world, he opens up his ear to the life within. Reeling, we see him elevated far above our sphere; his feeblest path is for us a new flight.

He dominates and reconciles what is strange and incompatible. He feels through his mind; he thinks through his heart. He teaches us new jubilation, new laments, new prayer and new jests.

We have come to commemorate his death, our sacred tears, alas, all that is left to us. We have seen him – the veil of the tomb is ripped asunder – and the funeral rite becomes a feast of life!

He lives! He who claims he is dead lies! Like the Sun, which comes and enchants and illuminates and, its day's work done, leaves us, thus did he come; and thus he has returned home.

He lives! for his life is his music; no god will ever uproot that from the world's breast. It will be passed on to our grandchildren and great-grandchildren, who will surely be more deeply inspired by it than even their ancestors.

He lives! You saw him, heard him, and now hear him once more. My dull wreath will fade; the one celebration worthy to honor him he has created himself through his own song!

In addition, a poem by Baron von Schlechta was distributed, and further:

AT BEETHOVEN'S FUNERAL

on March 29, 1827

by I. F. Castelli[194]

Ev'ry tear that is shed by the mourner is holy;
  When the dust of the mighty to earth is resigned,

When those he held dearest move sadly and slowly
  To the grave of the friend in whose heart they were shrined:–

But our grief-stricken train is a wild sea that surges,
  That spreads to yon starry pavilion o'erhead
And girdles the globe: for all nature sings dirges,
  Where'er rings an echo, to-day o'er the dead.

But weep not for him: for yourselves sorrow only:
  Though proud was his place in the hierarchy here,
This earth might not hold him; his spirit was lonely,
  And yearned for a home in a loftier sphere.

So Heaven to the minstrel its portals uncloses:
  The Muse thither calls him, to sit by her side
And hear, from the throne where in bliss she reposes,
  His own hallow'd harmonies float far and wide.

Yet here, in our memories homed, he abideth;
  Round his name lives a glory that ne'er may grow dim;
Time fain would o'ertake him, but Time he derideth;
  The grisly Destroyer is distanced by him.

Immediately after the burial an event full of foreboding took place. Franz Schubert, Benedict Randhartinger, and Franz Lachner went to the inn "Zur Mehlgrube" on the Neue Markt. They ordered wine, and Schubert raised his glass with the toast: "To the memory of our immortal Beethoven!" and when the glasses were emptied, he filled his glass again and cried out: "And now to the first of us to follow Beethoven!"[195] And he was a prophet of his own death: on November 19, 1828, that musical genius died, of whom Beethoven said on his deathbed: "Truly, Schubert has the divine spark."[196] And now, five graves to the side, and above his great exemplar, he too found the resting place he had hoped for, in his feverish wanderings, "next to Beethoven."

A few days after the funeral, on April 3, the requiem mass was sung. Mozart's immortal Requiem was to be sung for the even more immortal Beethoven in the Court parish church of the Augustinian monks, with the Italian singers taking part. However, Barbaja, the impresario, had signed a contract which forbade his singers to appear in public outside the theater, under a penalty of 200 gulden. But the incomparable Lablache, in his enthusiasm for the departed, said flatly that he would sing, and sent the 200 gulden to Barbaja.[197] The church could hardly contain the crowds who came.

My father and I stood next to Canova's memorial to Christina, said to be the spot with the best acoustics in the church.[198] No one will ever hear the Dies irae sung again as it was that day; never will there be a more inspired performance of the Requiem. Lablache's voice to the trumpet accompaniment, the feelings aroused by the occasion – everything had a shattering effect.

On April 5 Cherubini's Requiem was sung in the Karlskirche in a second mass.

That made it all the more painful for us, only a few days later, in the same month of April, to see the rooms in the Schwarzspanierhaus, which were sacred for us, desecrated by the auction of the house furnishings and Beethoven's belongings. A miserable collection of old-clothes dealers had found their way in, and the articles of clothing that came under the hammer were tugged this way and that, the pieces of furniture pushed and thumped, everything disarranged and soiled. My father, who had been ill several times during Beethoven's illness (as the conversation books show), forced himself to be present, and to follow the proceedings vigorously, "so that there shouldn't be any cheating." I went with him. It weighed heavily on our hearts. My father purchased, on his own account, the little black box and the yellow one, which we had so often handed to Beethoven in his bed.[199] For his friend, Court Councillor Baron Neustädter, he bought the writing desk that stood in the ante-chamber, to the left of the entrance hall, along with a stand from the bedroom (after Baron Neustädter's death, it came into my possession). He bought up the serving ladle for my piano teacher Anton Heller; Heller had engraved on it on one side "A. H." and on the other "L. van Beethoven, died March 26, 1827"; after his death it too came into my possession.[200] The Graf piano was taken back by the manufacturer. The Broadwood piano, which was put up for sale, was not purchased by my father because it went up only to C and did not meet the demands of the modern, that is Beethoven, era. The bookcase from the study must have been purchased by a Fräulein Annacker; for after her death it came into the possession of A. W. Thayer (see p. 66).

I also got the lithographic reproduction in a black frame, of the medal Beethoven received from Louis XVIII, a compass, and two portraits of women, one of which was recognized by Count Gallenberg, who is still living, as his mother (née Giulietta Guicciardi).[201]

As the result of these distressing scenes at the auction in the room where Beethoven had died, my father suffered a relapse, with an inflamed liver that soon confined him to his bed, and on June 4 of the same year, at midnight, the same hour of the night as his Julie, he followed his exalted friend into the beyond.

This made a total change in my situation. I was only fourteen and learned of the second auction, in November 1827, of the intellectual effects of Beethoven only after it was over. And so I have none of all the valuable manuscripts and autographs that got into other hands, always at low prices, sometimes ridiculously cheap; and all the more so because my father had strictly forbidden me to take even the smallest scrap of what Beethoven, when alive, would have given me by the armful if it had entered my mind to ask him for it.

A concert was organized in the hall of the Landstände in Vienna, playing exclusively compositions by the deceased, in order to erect a monument with the proceeds. In front of the monument there was, up to a few years ago, a little bush; individual leaves were plucked from it and must be spread all over the world, but the bush dried up a few years ago. The railing around the grave was added during the year of exhumation, 1863.[202]

For some years after the death of the great "brain owner," his brother, the "landowner," played a strange, naive role. During Ludwig's life Johann's interest in his works was limited to possible gain from them; now he tried to present himself as an appreciative admirer. At concert performances of music by his deceased brother he would sit in the first row, all got up in a blue frock coat with white vest, and loudly shriek Bravos from his big mouth, at the end of every piece, beating his bony white-gloved hands together importantly. These oversize gloves, with their flapping fingers, could often be seen elsewhere as well, in the elegant drives in the Prater, where Johann would drive a team of two, even more often four, solid, dark-brown, ornately harnessed horses, stiffly perched on the seat of an old-fashioned phaeton; or sometimes he would have himself driven, leaning back as if stretched out, with two servants in copious, if well-worn, gold braid sitting in the other seat of the carriage behind him. It was said of the two footmen that only one was the coachman, while the other one was a caretaker from his house in the Allee-gasse, dressed up for the occasion. It was also said that, contrary to usual practice, the harness and the two liveries, whose quality and tailoring would suggest they came from the flea market, were kept in Johann's vestibule. All this pretentiousness and in general the overall appearance of Johann (who bore no physical resemblance to Ludwig: he had a long face, big nose, one eye squinting outwards, giving his face an expression of perpetual self-satisfaction) earned him the nickname of "Archduke Lorenz," from the

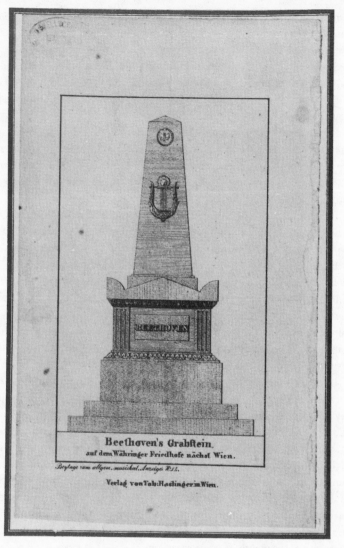

Beethoven's Grabstein.
auf dem Währinger Friedhofe nächst Wien.

Beylage zum allgem. musikal. Anzeige N:32.

Verlag von Tob: Haslinger in Wien.

PLATE 31   Beethoven's grave at Währing Cemetery.
Unsigned engraving sold by Tobias Haslinger

familiar proverb about people who endeavor to put on a great show and conduct themselves ridiculously in the process. Johann died in Vienna in January 1848. He proved to be as preposterous after his brother's death as he had been contemptible during his brother's life. His nephew Karl's widow has a portrait of him, a good likeness (see Plate 20).[203]

His repeatedly notorious sister-in-law, the widow of his brother Caspar Carl, died only a few years ago in Baden near Vienna.[204]

Of the family of their son, Beethoven's nephew Karl, – as already mentioned – his widow, a son Ludwig, and four respectable daughters are still alive; three of the daughters are married.[205] Thayer and I find a considerable resemblance to their immortal great-uncle in the features of the youngest (still unmarried) daughter.

In 1845 Bonn finally obtained a bronze statue of her great son from the artistic hand of Hähnel,[206] through the generous efforts of Franz Liszt. A bronze bust from Fernkorn's studio was erected on the "Beethovenweg" near Heiligenstadt (a Vienna suburb).[207] This led Josef Hellmesberger, our violin virtuoso and artistic director, to say, "The graves of Beethoven and Schubert were too much exposed to all kinds of disrespect," and as a result the management of the Vienna Gesellschaft der Musikfreunde set up a committee to examine the two graves, arriving at the conclusion: "the earthly remains of Beethoven and Schubert should be insured against further neglect."*

In connection with the exhumation and reinterment performed on this occasion (at which the members of my family resident in Vienna, as well as my son Gerhard and my younger sister Marie were present), I would like to add a few further medical remarks in passing, which are given less emphasis in the *Aktenmässige Darstellung*.[208] It was extremely interesting physiologically to compare the compact thickness of Beethoven's skull and the fine, almost feminine thinness of Schubert's, and to relate them, almost directly, to the character of their music. In addition, Beethoven's palate was found to have an exceptionally smooth surface and the upper teeth projected almost straight out horizontally; during his life this showed only in the forward protuberance of the mouth. It was also striking that the last lower left molar was found to have an excellent gold filling. This was unusual in two respects: In those days (the 1820s) it was exceptional to have such good fillings per-

---

* See *Aktenmässige Darstellung der Ausgrabung und Wieder-beisetzung der irdischen Reste von Beethoven und Schubert. Veranlaßt durch die Direktion der Gesellschaft der Musikfreunde des österreichische Kaiserstaates im Oktober 1863* (Vienna, 1863).

PLATE 32   Gerhard von Breuning, aged 70. Unsigned photograph

formed, and further, it was surprising that Beethoven was able to endure the operation, which always requires such patience. The skulls of Beethoven and Schubert were photographed on this occasion by J. B. Rottmayer (now in Trieste) and plaster casts were made by sculptor Wittman (now in Schwechat, near Vienna). Beethoven's skull shows some missing teeth, whereas none were missing during his lifetime; the reason for this is that during the exhumation some teeth were not found. – All this was done in the course of nine days, October 13 to 22. As a member of the board of the Gesellschaft der Musikfreunde I had the custody of Beethoven's skull on their behalf, as my colleague, Dr. Standthartner, had custody of Schubert's. What stormy feelings passed through my mind evoking such powerful memories, as I had possession of that head for a few days, cleaned from it bits of dirt, took plaster casts of the base of the skull for Professor Romeo Seligmann, kept it by my bedside overnight, and in general proudly watched over that head from whose mouth, in years gone by, I had so often heard the living word!

During Beethoven's lifetime many, even the majority of his most important works were not understood and put on one side; we need only think of the fate of the Violin Concerto, the Mass in D, yes, even the Ninth Symphony and *Fidelio*, etc. etc., not to speak of the last quartets, which people for years called the "crazy" quartets.[209] It was only long after his death, in the early 1840s, through the untiring efforts of an Otto Nicolai, Josef Hellmesberger, Frau Clara Schumann, Johann Herbeck, Otto Dessoff, and others, that repeated performances of these masterworks brought Vienna to understand and appreciate the sublime significance of Beethoven's Muse and the brilliant harmony of his compositions.[210] Josef Hellmesberger has recently brought a new jewel into the constellation of the master's works, by his discovery and splendid performance of the first movement of a second violin concerto (in the archives of the Vienna Gesellschaft der Musikfreunde),[211] which goes some way to reward the never satisfied audience.

EDITOR'S NOTES

Editor's introduction

1 See Kerst, II, pp. 50–51, 163–175; Albert Leitzmann, ed., *Ludwig van Beethoven: Berichte der Zeitgenossen, Briefe und persönliche Aufzeichnungen*, 2 vols. (Leipzig, 1921), I, 323–334; Sonneck, pp. 196–206; Jacques-Gabriel Prod'homme, ed., *Beethoven: Raconté par ceux qui l'ont vu* (Paris, 1927), pp. 213–226.

2 Wilhelm Thöny, *Beethoven-Zyklus. Zeichnungen zu Breunings 'Erinnerungen aus dem Schwarzspanierhause,'* ed. Wolfgang Schneditz (Vienna, 1954).

3 Breuning, *Aus dem Schwarzspanierhause*, 2nd edn., ed. Alfred Christlieb Kalischer (Berlin and Leipzig, 1907). Reprinted Hildesheim, 1970. Theodor Frimmel, noting Kalischer's failure to correct Breuning's numerous mistakes and his introduction of new ones, concluded that the second edition is, "as it stands, simply superflous." *BJ* II (1909), p. 351.

4 For Beethoven and the Breunings, see the various editions of Thayer; Wegeler-Ries; Ludwig Schiedermair, *Der junge Beethoven* (Leipzig, 1925), pp. 173–179, 197–208, 301–309; Frimmel, *Handbuch*, I, pp. 64–68, Joseph Schmidt-Görg, entry, "Gerhard von Breuning," *MGG*, XV, p. 1080; and the various editions of Breuning.

5 Beethoven's Konversationshefte, Heft 131, fol. 3v–4r (Deutsche Staatsbibliothek in der Stiftung Preussischer Kulturbesitz). This and the following conversation-book entries are cited from the as-yet-unpublished final volume of Köhler–Herre–Beck by the generous permission of the Deutscher Verlag für Musik. I am grateful to Grita Herre of the Deutsche Staatsbibliothek for providing copies of the transcriptions. The entry is also published in Kalischer, "Beethovens 'Ariel' and 'Hosenknopf,'" in *Beethoven und seine Zeitgenossen*, 4 vols. (Berlin, n.d. [1908–1910]), IV, pp. 273–289 (here p. 279). See also Stephan Ley, "Ein Dreizehn-jähriger an Beethovens letztem Krankenlager," in *Aus Beethovens Erdentagen* (Bonn, 1948), pp. 224–231.

6 Heft 127, fol. 21r–21v; Kalischer, "Beethovens 'Ariel' und 'Hosenknopf,'" p. 277.

7 Heft 128, fol. 9v–10v; Kalischer, "Beethovens 'Ariel' und 'Hosenknopf,'" pp. 278–279.

8 Heft 137, 12r–14r; Kalischer, "Beethovens 'Ariel' und 'Hosenknopf,'" pp. 280, 282.

9 Heft 137, 21r–22r; 23r; 27r; Kalischer, "Beethovens 'Ariel' und 'Hosenknopf,'"
  pp. 282–283.
10 Heft 137, 2r.
11 Heft 136, 47v–48r. Kalischer, "Beethovens 'Ariel' und 'Hosenknopf,'" p. 287.
12 Only a handful of Breuning's entries were published during his lifetime and none
  prior to publication of his book. See Ludwig Nohl, *Beethovens Leben*, 3 vols. in 4
  (Vienna, 1864; Leipzig, 1867–1877), III, pp. 769, 771, 957 note 327. But it is
  surprising that Breuning did not cite the conversation books which he apparently
  consulted at the Berlin Royal Library.
13 See Alan Tyson, "Ferdinand Ries (1784–1838): The History of his Contribution
  to Beethoven Biography," *Nineteenth-Century Music*, 7 (1984), 209–221.
14 Max Unger, "Beethovens Konversationshefte als biographische Quelle," *Musik
  im Kriege*, Nos. 11–12 (February–March 1944), 209–215 (here, 211). Donald W.
  MacArdle, "Anton Felix Schindler, Friend of Beethoven," *Music Review*, 24
  (1963), 50–74 (here, 53).
15 See Solomon, *Beethoven Essays*, pp. 126–138; Solomon, "The Rochlitz Anecdotes:
  Issues of Authenticity in Early Mozart Biography," in *Mozart Studies*, ed. Cliff
  Eisen (Oxford, 1991), pp. 1–59.
16 Eduard Hüffer, *Anton Felix Schindler, der Biograph Beethovens* (Münster, 1909),
  p. 17; Wilhelm Lütge, "Anton Schindler (Briefe Schindlers über 3 Stücke aus der
  'Leonore,' Schottische usw. Lieder und die deutschen Texte zur C-Dur messe),"
  Der Bär: Jahrbuch von Breitkopf & Härtel (Leipzig, 1927), pp. 110–121 (here,
  p. 113).
17 Dagmar Beck and Grita Herre, "Anton Schindlers fingierte Eintragungen in den
  Konversationsheften," *Zu Beethoven: Aufsätze und Annotationen*, ed. Harry Gold-
  schmidt (Berlin, 1979), pp. 11–89; idem, "Einige Zweifel an der Überlieferung
  der Konversationshefte," *Bericht über den Internationalen Beethoven-Kongress
  Berlin 1977*, ed. Goldschmidt et al. (Leipzig, 1978), pp. 257–274. See also Peter
  Stadlen, "Schindler's Beethoven Forgeries," *Musical Times*, 118 (1977), 549–552;
  Stadlen, "Schindler and the Conversation Books," *Soundings*, no. 7 (1978), 2–18.
  A. B. Marx noted diplomatically that several dates given in an entry by Schindler
  "do not harmonize with the accustomed ones." See Marx, *Ludwig van Beethoven.
  Leben und Schaffen*, 2 vols. (2nd ed., Berlin, 1862), II, p. 209. As early as 1845,
  Holz described Schindler as using "*forged* or *stolen* conversation books, and *un-
  sophisticated evidence ...*" Thayer–Deiters–Riemann, V, p. 190; Thayer–Krehbiel,
  III, p. 198. Krehbiel openly charged Schindler with forgery of several conversation book entries: "There are mutilations, interlineations, and erasures in the
  Conversation Books which it is difficult to believe were not made for the purpose
  of bolstering up mistaken statements in his biography ..." Thayer–Krehbiel, III,
  p. 281; see also III, p. 273, and I, p. 321n.
18 Kerman, "Schindler's Beethoven," *Musical Times*, 108 (1967), 40.

19 Hüffer, p. 73.

20 Schindler, in *Frankfurter Konversationsblatt*, July 14, 1842, see Thayer–Deiters–Riemann, v, p. 447. However, at the time of Beethoven's illness, Schindler reported in a conversation book of January 1827 on Wawruch's favorable reputation and noted how "famous and treasured he is by his students." Ley, *Aus Beethovens Erdentagen*, p. 212.

21 Moscheles, I, pp. 146–147. Soon after Beethoven's death, in a letter to Moscheles of April 11, 1827, Schindler first related his account of the doctor's supposed perfidy, concluding: "In short, to you, I can and will say it; Beethoven might have lived ten years longer, had he not been sacrificed to the most contemptible meanness and ignorance of others. All these matters will be more fully explained at a later period." Moscheles, I, pp. 175–176.

22 Dr. Wawruch, in Sonneck, p. 225.

23 Thayer's notebooks, see Henry Edward Krehbiel, *Music & Manners in the Classical Period* (Westminster, 1898), p. 206.

24 Frimmel, *Handbuch*, p. 75; Max Vancsa, "Nachträgliches zur Biographie Karls van Beethoven," *Die Musik*, I, part 2 (1901–1902), pp. 1083–1084 (here, p. 1084). See also Vancsa, "Beethovens Neffen," in Supplement to *Munich Allgemeine Zeitung*, 6–7 (1901).

25 Thayer, *Ein kritischer Beitrag zur Beethoven-Literatur* (Berlin, 1877), p. 28. Breuning was stung into drafting an intemperate and feeble response, which fortunately was not published during his lifetime. "It is clear how completely Thayer has been taken in by Johann's conduct," he wrote: "For there is an essential difference between using a carriage and ludicrous ostentation ..." Rudolf Klein, "Gerhard von Breuning über Beethovens Beziehung zu seinen Verwandten. Ein unbekannter Entwurf zu einem Artikel," *Österreichische Musikzeitschrift*, 29 (1974), 67–75 (here, 74).

26 Thayer observes that Breuning virtually omits Holz. See Thayer–Deiters–Riemann, v, p. 187. Schindler would have us believe that Holz took "his departure" from Beethoven in December 1826: this is "an exaggeration," writes Thayer. See Thayer–Deiters–Riemann, v, p. 191.

27 Schindler–MacArdle, pp. 319–320. Krehbiel notes that there are more entries by Johann in the conversation books for the first two months of 1827 than for any other individual. Thayer–Krehbiel, III, p. 295.

28 Letter to Wegeler, December 7, 1826, Anderson III, p. 1321 (letter 1542).

29 See Wegeler–Ries, Supplement, pp. 22–23; Wegeler–Ries Eng. edn., p. 158.

30 Frimmel, *Handbuch*, I, p. 67.

31 "Die Schädel Beethovens und Schuberts," *Neue Freie Presse*, September 17, 1886, reprinted in Kalischer, pp. 209–221; "Aus Beethovens Konversationsheften," *Neue Freie Presse*, Dec. 30, 1886, reprinted in Kalischer, pp. 191–208; "Drei bisher unveröffentlichte Briefe Beethovens," *Neue Freie Presse*, December 30, 1887.

Memories of Beethoven: From the House of the Black-Robed Spaniards

1 Wegeler–Ries, Supplement, p. 28; Wegeler–Ries Eng. edn., p. 163.

2 Prince Nikolaus Esterházy (1765–1833). From late October 1822 until May 17, 1823 Beethoven lived at Obere Pfarrgasse at the corner of the Kothgasse in the suburb of Windmühle; he lived briefly in the Inner City on the Krugerstrasse in April–May 1825; and from October 15, 1825 until his death he lived in the Schwarzspanierhaus at 15 Schwarzspanierstrasse. See Smolle, *Wohnstätten*, pp. 73–85 passim, 135–136; Rudolf Klein, *Beethoven Stätten in Österreich* (Vienna, 1970), pp. 122, 142, 145–149.

3 Wegeler–Ries gives the date incorrectly; the correct date is December 7, 1826. See Anderson, III, p. 1321 (letter 1542).

4 Emanuel Josef v. Breuning (1740–1777).

5 The Hatzfeld family was influential in Bonn cultural life during Beethoven's youth. He dedicated his Variations on Righini's "Venni amore," WoO 65, to Countess Maria Anna Hatzfeld. Austrian statesman Prince Metternich (1773–1859).

6 Anon., *Ludwig van Beethoven. ein dramatisches Charakterbild in vier Aufzügen mit einem Epilog zur Feier von Beethovens hundertjährigem Geburtstage am 16. Dezember 1870. By a Resident of Bonn* (Leipzig, 1870). See Hans Volkmann, "Beethoven-dramen," *Die Musik*, 5, part 1 (November 1905), pp. 258–268 (here, pp. 263–264).

7 Christof (1771–1841); Eleonore (1772–1841); Stephan (1774–1827); Lorenz (1777–1798). Breuning spells his father's name variously "Steffen," "Stefan," and "Stephan."

8 Heribert Rau, *Beethoven. Kulturhistorischer Roman*, 4 vols. (Leipzig, 1859); 2nd edn. as *Beethoven. Ein Kunstlerleben culturhistorischbiographisch geschildert*, 4 vols. (Leipzig, 1869); Wolfgang Müller von Königswinter, *Furioso*, in *Westermann's Illustrirte Deutsche Monatshefte*, 9 (1860–1861), nos. 49–51 (October–December, 1860), 1–22, 121–138, and 234–267; Eng. translation as *Furioso, or Passages from the Life of Ludwig van Beethoven* (Cambridge, 1865), in which, although a novel, it is described as "abridged from the diary of F. C. [!] Wegeler"; G. Mensch, *Ludwig van Beethoven. Ein musikalisches Charakterbild* (Leipzig, 1871).

9 The Beethoven monument on the Münsterplatz was designed by the Dresden sculptor Ernst Julius Hähnel (1811–1891); its inauguration was celebrated by a Beethoven festival in Bonn in August 1845.

10 Beethoven's childhood friend, the physician Franz Gerhard Wegeler (1765–1848). The starting date of Wegeler's friendship with Beethoven remains open: Wegeler gave it as 1782 (Wegeler-Ries, p. xi; Wegeler-Ries Eng. ed., p. 4), but Thayer wanted to assign it to late 1787. Thayer, I, 169–71; see Thayer-Forbes, p. 85.

11 Contrary to Schindler's assertion, the quotation is not from any Beethoven letter. See Schindler–MacArdle, p. 47.

12 See Wegeler–Ries, p. 3; Wegeler–Ries Eng. Edn., p. 9; Thayer–Forbes, pp. 53–54. See also Stephan Ley, "Zu Beethovens Geburtstag," *NBJ*, 7 (1937), 29–31. Beethoven's correct birth-year was published before Thayer by Wilhelm Christian Müller, "Etwas über Ludwig van Beethoven," *AMZ*, 29 (1827), col. 345; Wegeler–Ries, pp. 3–4; Wegeler–Ries Eng. edn., p. 9; Schindler–Moscheles, p. 9; and others.

13 The present address is 18 Bonngasse.

14 Franz Anton Ries (1755–1846) and his sons the composer-pianist Ferdinand Ries (1784–1838) and the composer-violinist Hubert Ries (1802–1886).

15 The spider story was first published in *AMZ*, 2 (1799–1800), col. 653 and was shown by Johann Aloys Schlosser to have arisen from a confusion of Beethoven's name with that of the French violinist Isidor Bertheaume, of whom the story was first told by Disjonval. See Schlosser, *Ludwig van Beethoven's Biographie* (Prague, 1828) [1827]}, pp. 9–10. See also Schindler–MacArdle, pp. 38–39.

16 Federigo Fiorillo, *36 Caprices*, op. 3.

17 Gerhard von Kügelgen (1772–1820) and Karl Ferdinand von Kügelgen (1772–1832). See Frimmel, *Handbuch*, I, pp. 311–312; Friedrich Christian A. Hasse, *Das Leben Gerhard's v. Kügelgen. Nebst einigen Nachrichten aus dem Leben des k. russischen Cabinetsmalers Karl v. Kügelgen* (Leipzig, 1824).

18 The German classicist Johann Joachim Winckelmann (1717–1767).

19 Three Clavier Sonatas (*Electoral*), WoO 47, published at Speier in 1783, with a dedicatory letter dated October 14, 1783. See Anderson, III, pp. 1410–11 (Appendix D, 1). It was Maximilian Franz (1756–1801), the successor to Maximilian Friedrich (1708–1784) as Elector, who was the brother of Emperor Joseph II.

20 With the support of his teacher, composer and court organist Christian Gottlob Neefe (1748–1798), Beethoven was appointed assistant court organist in 1782. Beethoven's important patron Count Ferdinand Waldstein (1762–1823) did not arrive in Bonn until 1788. Breuning takes over this error from Wegeler–Ries, p. 13; Wegeler–Ries Eng. edn., p. 20. Much of the information in the remainder of Breuning's paragraph also derives from Wegeler–Ries.

21 Wegeler–Ries, pp. 14–15; Wegeler–Ries Eng. edn., pp. 20–21. Bonn court-tenor Ferdinand Heller. See Joseph Schmidt–Görg, "Ein neuer Fund in den Skizzenbüchern Beethovens: die Lamentationen des Propheten Jeremias," *BJ 1957/58* (Bonn, 1959), pp. 107–110.

22 Wegeler–Ries, pp. 42–43, 58–59. Wegeler–Ries Eng. edn., pp. 42–43, 55. Anna Barbara (Babette) Koch-Belderbusch (1771–1807). The name of the heroine of Beethoven's opera – which he intended to entitle *Leonore* – was not inspired by Eleonore von Breuning. Beethoven's libretto derives from J. N. Bouilly's *Léonore ou L'amour conjugal*, set to music by Pierre Gaveaux in 1799.

23 Beethoven and Haydn probably also met during Christmas 1790 when Haydn stopped in Bonn on the way to England.

24 Beethoven arrived in Vienna on April 7, 1787, and departed around April 20; his trip was cut short, among other reasons, by his mother's illness. His journey to Vienna was considered a failure; there is no evidence that he was received by the Viennese nobility. See Martin Staehelin, "Beethovens Brief an den Freiherrn von Schaden von 1787," *Jahresgabe 1982 des Vereins Beethoven-Haus*, no. 1 (Bonn, 1982), pp. 11–13; Eduard Panzerbieter, "Beethovens erste Reise nach Wien …," *Zeitschrift für Musikwissenschaft*, 10 (1927–1928), 153–161.

25 Emperor Joseph II reigned from 1780 until his death in 1790. For Hunczovsky, see note 31 below.

26 The Mozart anecdote is first published in Ignaz Ritter von Seyfried, *Ludwig van Beethoven's Studien* (Vienna, 1832), Supplement, p. 4, note. It is repeated by Beethoven's friend, the violinist Karl Holz, who told Mozart's biographer Otto Jahn (1813–1869): "As a child he was taken to Mozart, who asked him to play, whereupon he improvised. 'That was very pretty,' said Mozart, 'but studied.' Beethoven thereupon asked him for a theme and improvised in such a manner that Mozart said to several friends: 'Pay attention to this one, he will have something to tell us.'" Kerst, II, p. 185.

27 Beethoven's mother, Maria Magdalena Keverich Leym, was born December 19, 1746, and therefore died at the age of 40.

28 See note 17.

29 Nottebohm, *Beethoveniana* was published by C. F. Peters of Leipzig. Beethoven's souvenir album (*Stammbuch*) is transcribed on pp. 138–144; the entry by Anna Maria Koch, née Klemmer (1749–1817), is on p. 139. See the facsimile edition, *Die Stammbücher Beethovens und der Babette Koch*, ed. Max Braubach (Bonn, 1970).

30 *Briefwechsel zwischen Goethe und Zelter*, ed. Friedrich Wilhelm Riemer, 6 vols. (Berlin, 1833–1834). Karl Friedrich Zelter (1758–1832) was a noted Berlin composer. He did not favor Beethoven's music.

31 Johann Nepomuk Hunczovsky (1752–1798), physician, scholar, and art connoisseur. See Frimmel, *Handbuch*, I, p. 230. Lorenz von Breuning wrote to his sister in 1795: "We also often gather at Hunczovsky's, one of my teachers." Ley, *Beethoven als Freund*, p. 250.

32 Brownianism (or Brunonianism), a philosophy of medicine formulated by the Scottish physician John Brown (1735–1788), had a wide vogue in Austria and Germany at the close of the eighteenth century. Among its partisans were Beethoven's doctor, Anton Braunhofer (see note 157 below), who called himself "a quasi student of Brown" (Köhler–Herre–Beck, VII, p. 229), and the noted Viennese physician Johann Peter Frank (1745–1821), father of Beethoven's friend Joseph Frank (1771–1842). See also Anderson, III, p. 1196 (letter 1371).

33 The letter is entered in Lorenz von Breuning's souvenir album. Anderson, I, p. 27 (letter 21). The opening quotation is from Schiller's *Don Carlos*, Act IV, scene 21.

34 For further excerpts from this letter, including Lorenz von Breuning's remark, "I

once was certain that I could not be friends with him," see Ley, *Beethoven als Freund*, p. 250.

35 Thayer, p. 174; Thayer–Krehbiel, I, p. 99, note 1. Thayer's first editor, Hermann Deiters, agreed with Breuning that Beethoven's association with the Breuning family began much earlier. See Thayer–Deiters, I, p. 210.

36 On June 21, 1893, Beethoven's remains were removed to the Central Cemetery in Vienna; on June 1, 1893, Stephan von Breuning's remains were removed to the Breuning family vault in the Central Cemetery.

37 Gerhard von Vering (1755–1823).

38 Beethoven took rooms at the Rothes Haus in the Alservorstädter Glacis in about May 1804. At first he had his own quarters but soon he moved into Breuning's rooms, where he remained until they quarrelled in July. In mid-July Beethoven asked Ries to find him new lodgings. See letter of July 14, 1804, in Anderson, I, p. 111 (letter 92). See Smolle, *Wohnstätten*, pp. 27–28; Klein, *Beethoven Stätten in Österreich*, pp. 37–38.

39 Translation amended from Thayer–Forbes, p. 358. Beethoven did not remain in the Rothes Haus until November: he left Breuning's lodgings in July, when he moved to Baden for the summer; upon his return to Vienna around the beginning of October, he took new lodgings in the Pasqualatihaus in the Mölkerbastei.

40 Beethoven's landlord was his friend Baron Johann Baptist von Pasqualati (1777–1830), dedicatee of the Elegischer Gesang, Op. 118. Beethoven remained in the Pasqualatihaus from fall 1804 until the spring of 1815, with two interruptions (1808 to 1810; February to June 1814). Smolle, *Wohnstätten*, p. 50.

41 Julie von Vering (1791–1809). In later years, Beethoven told the Giannatasio family about "one of his friends, who loved the same girl as he did, but the girl preferred Beethoven. Perhaps from an excess of generosity Beethoven always withdrew, leaving the field to his friend. But the girl did not live very long. I believe she died soon after marrying his friend." Memoirs of Fanny Giannatasio del Rio, in Jacques-Gabriel Prod'homme, ed., *Beethoven: Raconté par ceux qui l'ont vu* (Paris, 1927), p. 89.

42 The composer Johann Schenk (1753–1836) became acquainted with Beethoven shortly after the latter's arrival in Vienna; he helped Beethoven with his counterpoint exercises for Haydn.

43 Both the Concerto for Violin and Orchestra in D major, Op. 61, and the arrangement of it for piano and orchestra were published in August 1808 by the Viennese publisher, the Bureau des Arts et d'Industrie. The former bore a dedication "à son ami, Monsieur de Breuning, Secrétaire Aulique au service de Sa Majesté l'Empereur d'Autriche," and the latter a dedication "à Madame de Breuning." (Later impressions added the words, "née noble de Wering." The English edition, published by Clementi in 1810, lacks a dedication. Franz Clement (1780–1842), for whom the Violin Concerto was composed, was a leading Viennese violinist and conductor.

44 The complete text of Czerny's "Erinnerungen aus meinem Leben" was published as "Recollections from my Life," translated by Ernest Sanders, in *Musical Quarterly*, 42 (1956), 302–317.

45 Anonymous letter of April 11, 1799, "Die berühmtesten Klavierspielerinnen und Klavierspieler Wiens," *AMZ*, 1 (1798–1799), col. 525.

46 Their remains were transferred to the family vault in the Central Cemetery in 1893.

47 Beethoven wrote to Breitkopf & Härtel, on February 19, 1811: "I wanted to go to Italy at the beginning of the winter ... " Anderson, 1, p. 314 (letter 297).

48 For Breuning's role in the 1806 version of *Fidelio*, including his abridgement and revision of the 1805 libretto, see Thayer–Forbes, pp. 393–398.

49 It actually had only two performances, on March 29 and April 10, 1806; a scheduled third performance, on April 12, was cancelled.

50 Beethoven's lied, "Als die Geliebte sich trennen wollte" (also published as "Empfindungen bei Lydiens Untreue"), WoO 132, was composed in the summer of 1806 to Breuning's text, a free translation from F. B. Hoffmann's libretto for Jean-Pierre Solié's opera *Le Secret*.

51 Stephan von Breuning has the titles reversed: Beethoven expected that *Leonore* would be used as the title for the 1806 performances.

52 Gerold was a Viennese publisher of the later nineteenth century. The reference here is unclear.

53 The reference is to Beethoven's patron, Prince Karl Lichnowsky (1756–1814). The Berlin performances did not materialize.

54 *Fidelio* was frequently staged in Vienna after its great success in 1814, including highly-acclaimed revivals in 1819, 1822, and 1826. The famous German tenor, Aloys Ander (1821–1864).

55 The correspondent for the *Weiner Theaterzeitung* paraphrased two reviews in *The Illustrated London News*, 18, no. 487 (May 24, 1851), 448–449, and No. 489 (May 31, 1851), 484–485. The principal singers mentioned include the French soprano Jeanne Anaïs Castellan (1819–after 1858); the German soprano Jeanne Sophie Charlotte Cruvelli (1826–1907); the Italian baritone Filippo Coletti (1811–1894); the German bass Johann Karl Formès (1816–1889); the English tenor John Sims Reeves (1818–1900); the German tenor George Stigelli (*c.* 1820–1868); the Italian-French bass Joseph Dieudonné Tagliafico (1821–1900); and the Italian tenor Enrico Tamberlik (1820–1899). Others mentioned include the Italian Enrico Calzolari (1823–1888); the Italian bass Pietro Ferranti (1825–1896); the Italian bass Federico Lablache (*c.* 1815–1887); the Italian tenor Italo Gardoni (1821–1882); and the French baritone Eugène Massol. The two productions were led by the celebrated opera composer and conductor Michael William Balfe (1808–1870) and the eminent conductor and composer Sir Michael Costa (1806–1884).

56 At this point Kalischer has added the following text from Breuning's notes: "Also from this time dates a gift by Beethoven to my mother, a small crocheted purse

which he once received from Henriette Sontag. Repeatedly up until just before his death he would say to my mother that he very much regretted that he never married." Kalischer, p. 53. Beethoven first got to know the famous singer Sontag (1806–1854) in 1822.

57 In a memo to Thayer, Breuning's sister Marie transmits similar reports from her mother concerning his attitudes towards love and marriage and her belief that Beethoven was courting her. See "Several Verbal Communications from my Mother Constanze von Breuning," in Thayer–Deiters–Riemann, v, pp. 255–256; Thayer–Forbes, pp. 967–968. "Ein Engel Leonore" is from Florestan's aria in Act II of *Fidelio*. The remaining quotations are from Schiller's "An die Freude"; the second line was used in the finale of *Fidelio*.

58 The plaster life-mask of Beethoven was made by the sculptor Franz Klein (?1779–?1840), who subsequently used it as a model for a famous bronzed plaster bust of Beethoven (Beethovenhaus, Bonn).

59 The closing quotation is from Schlosser's *Ludwig van Beethoven's Biographie*, p. 46.

60 Nottebohm, *Beethoveniana*, chapter 28, pp. 145–153, reprints passages about Beethoven from Weissenbach's *Meine Reise zum Kongress in Wien: Wahrheit und Dichtung* (Vienna, 1816).

61 *Wellingtons Sieg, oder die Schlacht bei Vittoria*, Op. 91 (1813).

62 This spurious anecdote appeared in Schindler–Moscheles, pp. 78–79, but was omitted from later editions, probably because the autograph of the Kyrie of the Missa solemnis is intact (Staatsbibliothek Preussischer Kulturbesitz, Berlin). There is a facsimile of the Kyrie, ed. Wilhelm Virneisel (Tutzing, 1965). Schindler evidently fabricated this anecdote to explain how he came to possess the original score of the Ninth Symphony. Schindler–Moscheles, p. 93, note.

63 Adapted from Schindler–MacArdle, pp. 229, 264.

64 This anecdote was told by Beethoven's acquaintance, the Bohemian composer Jan Emanuel Doležálek (1780–1858). Kerst, II, p. 192.

65 Beethoven is said to have thrown imperfect eggs at his housekeeper (see Seyfried, in Sonneck, p. 42); Ries told of Beethoven throwing a gravy-laden dish at a waiter at the Schwan Inn (Wegeler–Ries, pp. 121–122; Wegeler–Ries Eng. edn., pp. 108–109); in a communication from Holz to Thayer which was in Breuning's effects, Holz wrote, "Midday and evenings he ate at the Rothen Hahn; in the evenings he always ate soft-boiled eggs which, if they weren't the proper degree of hardness, he not rarely would throw at the waiter." See Ley, *Beethoven als Freund*, p. 254.

66 For the inns, wineshops, restaurants, and coffee-houses frequented by Beethoven, see Frimmel, "Beethoven als Gasthausbesucher in Wien," *NBJ*, I (1924), pp. 128–141; see also Frimmel, *Handbuch*, I, pp. 159–160. Schuppanzigh's quartet gave recitals at the small hall connected with the inn "Zum roten Igel"; the String

Quartet in E-flat major, Op. 127, had its premiere there. According to Holz, Beethoven waited at a neighboring tavern for a report on the reception of the B-flat Quartet, Op. 130. Wilhelm von Lenz, *Beethoven: Eine Kunst-Studie*, 6 vols (Kassel and Hamburg, 1855–1860), VI, pp. 218–219.

67 The reference is to "König Ottokars Glück und Ende" (1825) by the Austrian dramatist Franz Grillparzer (1791–1872). The account of Grillparzer receiving the news of Beethoven's decline and death closely parallels Grillparzer's published account in his "Erinnerungen an Beethoven" (1844–1845); see *Grillparzers sämtliche Werke*, ed. August Sauer, 20 vols (Stuttgart, n.d.), XX, p. 211.

68 From the fall of 1823 until early November 1824, Beethoven had lodgings in the house, "Zur schönen Sklavin," at the corner of Bockgasse no. 5 and Ungargasse. Smolle, *Wohnstätten*, p. 78.

69 In the summer of 1808, Beethoven and the Grillparzers lived in the same house in Heiligenstadt, in the Kirchengasse (now Grinzingerstrasse 64). Smolle, *Wohnstätten*, pp. 37–38.

70 Grillparzer told the same story to Thayer in 1861. Thayer, II, p. 104; Thayer–Deiters–Riemann, II, p. 178; Thayer–Forbes, p. 441.

71 The anecdotes about Grillparzer's mother and about the cab-fare are in *Grillparzers sämtliche Werke*, XX, pp. 206, 210–211. Admittedly, Breuning reinforced his memory on this occasion.

72 *Grillparzers sämtliche Werke*, XX, p. 210.

73 For the £100 from England, see note 165 below. In 1809, Beethoven was granted a lifetime annuity of 4000 florins by Archduke Rudolph, Prince Joseph Lobkowitz, and Prince Ferdinand Kinsky. Prince Karl Lichnowsky had provided Beethoven with a smaller annuity from about 1800 to about 1806.

74 Grillparzer's beloved friend Katherina Fröhlich (1800–1879). In the early fall of 1815, Beethoven took a summer lodging in Döbling in the house, "An der Stiege," next to Professor Jäger's house. See Klein, *Beethoven-Stätten*, pp. 83–84; Smolle, *Wohnstätten*, pp. 52, 133.

75 Hüffer writes that Breuning and Schindler, who had not met for thirty-two years, were together for four days. See Eduard Hüffer, *Anton Felix Schindler, der Biograph Beethovens* (Münster, 1909), p. 73.

76 "Bester Herr Graf, Sie sind ein Schaf!" WoO 183, composed February 20, 1823, for Beethoven's close friend, Count Moritz Lichnowsky (1771–1837), to whom he dedicated the Sonata, Op. 90.

77 No Beethoven letter contains the precise words "Datum, ohne zu geben," but he did sometimes use the very similar pun, "gegeben, ohne zu geben," as in a letter of January 28, 1826 to Bernhard Schotts Söhne: "Gegeben ohne was zu geben auf den Höhen von Schwarzspaniern (Given without giving anything on the heights of the Black Spaniards)." See Emerich Kastner and Julius Kapp, ed., *Ludwig van Beethovens sämtliche Briefe*, 2nd ed. (Leipzig, 1923), p. 803; Anderson, III, p. 1274

[letter 1466]; trans. from A. C. Kalischer, ed., *Beethoven's Letters*, translated by J. S. Shedlock (London, 1909), vol. II, p. 418.

78 Beethoven used this pun on the name Holz (wood) in several letters. "Most excellent wood of Christ," letters of August 10, 1825 and August 1826, in Anderson, III, pp. 1230 and 1296 (letters 1409 and 1500); "Most excellent Lignum Crucis!" letter of summer 1826, in Anderson, III, p. 1302 (letter 1512).

79 Anderson, I, p. 37, *c.* 1799 (letter 38).

80 See note 2 above.

81 The "Brainowner/Landowner" anecdote about Beethoven's brother Nikolaus Johann (1776–1848) was first published in 1840 in Schindler–Moschelès, p. 80. Prior to that time, Ries wrote to Wegeler: "I heard the anecdote about the Landowner and Brainowner several times; it is wholly innocuous, but, particularly if you knew the people involved, very good and appropriate.... However, it took place after my departure." Letter of August 6, 1837, see Ley, *Beethoven als Freund*, p. 265. Beethoven once addressed a letter "to Johann van Beethoven Landowner (Gutsbesitzer) in Gneixendorf." Letter of August 18, 1826, in *New Beethoven Letters*, ed. MacArdle and Ludwig Misch (Norman, 1957), p. 515.

82 Beethoven briefly took lodgings in Penzing in the Summer of 1824, not 1823; in the summer of 1823 he was first at Hetzendorf, then Baden. See Smolle, *Wohnstätten*, pp. 79–80, 75–78; Schindler–MacArdle, pp. 252–253, 263.

83 Between May 17 and August 13, 1823 Beethoven was in Hetzendorf at the Villa of Baron Sigismund Prónay von Tot-Prona, at 32 Haupstrasse. Smolle, *Wohnstätten*, pp. 75, 135.

84 This anecdote is expanded from Schindler–MacArdle, p. 263.

85 See Schindler–MacArdle, p. 382. Actually, three lodgings, and it was usual to rent a summer house while maintaining a winter residence.

86 See note 68 above.

87 For details of lodgings in 1824–1825, see Smolle, *Wohnstätten*, pp. 79–86, 135–136; see also note 2 above.

88 A friendly reference occurs in a letter to Ignaz Gleichenstein dated Feb. 28, 1811 (Anderson, I, p. 315 [letter 298]). The rupture therefore took place between 1811 and early 1815, the year which marks the onset of the mortal illness of Caspar Carl van Beethoven (1774–November 15, 1815). Apparently Beethoven and Stephan von Breuning met on occasion thereafter. There is only one passing reference to him in the correspondence between February 1811 and 1825, an undated letter (1817?) to Frau Nanette Streicher (Anderson, II, p. 736 [letter 866]). The letter of reconciliation (Anderson, I, pp. 118–119 [letter 98]) surely dates from the autumn of 1804. For discussions of the dating, see Kalischer, p. 11, note 3; MacArdle in Schindler–MacArdle, p. 357, note 48. Wegeler recalled another cooling between Stephan and von Breuning and Beethoven, citing Stephan's letter of January 10, 1809: "I haven't seen Beethoven for more than three months. During this time he

has written to me in a friendly way but I don't know why he has not come to see me." Wegeler–Ries, Supplement, p. 26; Wegeler–Ries Eng. edn., p. 161.

89 The miniature oil portrait on ivory was painted by the Danish artist Christian Hornemann (often spelled Horneman) (1765–1844) in 1803, not in 1802 as Breuning believed. Collection H. C. Bodmer, Beethovenhaus, Bonn.

90 Beethoven borrowed money from his dear friends Antonie Brentano (1780–1869) and Franz Brentano (1765–1844) probably in 1813 and 1814; the full amount was never repaid. See Solomon, *Beethoven Essays,* pp. 178, 180–181. See Schindler–MacArdle, p. 259.

91 Schindler–MacArdle, p. 99. The Oratorio, *Christus am Oelberge*, Op. 85.

92 The German-born Viennese sculptor, Anton Fernkorn (1813–1878); his Beethoven Monument (1863) is in Heiligenstadt Park, Vienna.

93 The sketches for the Tenth Symphony have been surveyed in Barry Cooper, "Newly Identified Sketches for Beethoven's Tenth Symphony," *Music & Letters*, 66 (1985), 9–18. See also note 165 below.

94 Wenzel Schlemmer (1760–1823) was Beethoven's main copyist for a quarter of a century. See Alan Tyson, "Notes on Five of Beethoven's Copyists," *Journal of the American Musicological Society,* 23 (1970), 440–444; Frimmel, *Handbuch*, I, pp. 120–121.

95 The famous piano virtuoso and composer Johann Nepomuk Hummel (1778–1837) and his wife Elisabeth, née Röckel (1793–1883). See also Ferdinand Hiller's account in Thayer–Forbes, pp. 1045–1046. There is no other indication that Beethoven had ever been in love with Frau Hummel. For Hummel's participation in the benefit concert for Schindler at the Josephstadt Theater, see Frimmel, *BJ*, I (1908), pp. 127–128. According to Hiller, Hummel improvised on the Allegretto of the A-major Symphony. See Thayer–Forbes, p. 1046. The concert program listed only one work by Beethoven, either his Overture to "The Ruins of Athens," Op. 113, or the Overture to "King Stephan," Op. 117. See Hüffer, *Schindler*, pp. 17–18.

96 The composer Giacomo Meyerbeer (1791–1864); the celebrated singer Karoline Unger (1803–1877); the naturalist and statesman Alexander von Humboldt (1769–1859). The collection of libretti and poems survives in DSB Berlin, autograph 37.

97 Grillparzer's *Melusine: Romantische Oper* was set by Conradin Kreutzer (1780–1849); first performance, Berlin, 1833.

98 *Homers Odüssee*, translated by Johann Heinrich Voss (Hamburg, 1781) and Christoph Christian Sturm, *Betrachtungen über die Werke Gottes im Reiche der Natur* (Reutlingen, 1811); Beethoven's marked copies of these books are in DSB, Berlin, autograph 40,2 and 40,3. The marked passages are reprinted in Ludwig Nohl, *Beethovens Brevier* (Leipzig, 1870) and in Leitzmann, ed., *Ludwig van Beethoven: Berichte der Zeitgenossen, Briefe und persönliche Aufzeichnungen*, II, pp. 267–289.

99 Jacob Hotschevar (dates not known), attorney for Johanna van Beethoven, became nephew Karl's guardian after Stephan von Breuning's death and was the guiding force in a projected but never completed "Vienna Biography" of Beethoven. See Solomon, *Beethoven Essays*, pp. 237–239. He apparently sought to recover numerous papers, books, autograph scores, conversation books, and memorabilia which Schindler appropriated after Beethoven's death and some of which he sold in 1845 to the Royal Library in Berlin for the sum of 2000 thalers and a lifetime annuity of 400 thalers. For details, see Hüffer, *Schindler*, pp. 52–55; Georg Schünemann, ed., *Ludwig van Beethoven: Konversationshefte*, 3 vols. (Berlin, 1941–1943), I, p. 7; see also MacArdle, "Anton Felix Schindler, Friend of Beethoven," *Music Review*, 24 (1963), 67–68. After Schindler's death, his estate descended to his sister, Marie Egloff (see note 103), who sold the remainder of his Beethoveniana to the Royal Library (Hüffer, *Schindler*, p. 75).

100 See Schindler–MacArdle, pp. 383, 507–508. All of these items, including ear-trumpets, monocle, spectacles, statuettes, hand-bell, brass seals, and cane, are now in the Beethovenhaus, Bonn. See *Verein Beethoven-Haus in Bonn. Bericht über die ersten fünfzehn Jahre seines Bestehens, 1889–1904* (Bonn, n.d. [1904]), pp. 66–67, with photograph following p. 66.

101 Act II, Terzett (No. 13).

102 Schindler was born 13 June 1795.

103 Schindler's sister was the former actress Marie Egloff. See Hüffer, *Schindler*, p. 75.

104 Beethoven moved from Baden into the Schwarzspanierhaus on October 15, 1825. The building was demolished in 1903–1904. Smolle, *Wohnstätten*, p. 84–85.

105 The Prussian Lieutenant General Baron Johann Heinrich von Minutoli (1772–1846), not Minutillo, according to Kalischer, p. 49, note.

106 The music-lover Fanny Linzbauer, née Tonsing, was a devotee of Beethoven's music. Her important interviews of Karl Holz in 1858 are in Ludwig Nohl, *Beethoven, Liszt, Wagner: Ein Bild der Kunstbewegung unseres Jahrhunderts* (Vienna, 1873), pp. 107–113. See note 131 below.

107 The portrait in oils of Ludwig van Beethoven the elder (1712–1773) by Leopold Radoux was painted in 1773. It is in the collection of Otto Reichert, Vienna.

108 Portrait in oils by Willibrord Josef Mähler, painted in 1804. Historisches Museum, Vienna.

109 The auction of Beethoven's manuscripts and music library was held on November 5, 1827, bringing 1140 florins 17 kreuzer. For the inventory, see Thayer–Forbes, pp. 1061–1070.

110 The String Quartets, Opp. 127, 130, 131, 132, and 135, the first three of which were commissioned by and dedicated to Prince Nikolas Boris Galitzin (1795–1866).

111 Pianist and composer Frédéric (Friedrich Wilhelm Michael) Kalkbrenner (1785–1849); pianist and composer Ignaz Moscheles (1794–1870); Thomas

Broadwood, of the London keyboard instrument manufacturer John Broadwood
and Sons. Breuning may have remembered the names of the donors incorrectly:
see Frimmel, *Beethoven Studien*, 2 vols. (Munich and Leipzig, 1905–1906), II,
pp. 226, 228.

112 Beethoven acknowledged receipt of the Broadwood piano on February 3, 1818.
Letter to Thomas Broadwood in Anderson, II, p. 755 (letter 891). It has a six-
octave range C¹–b³. It is presently in the National Museum, Budapest. See
Thayer–Forbes, pp. 694–696. For a photograph, see Frimmel, *Beethoven-
Studien*, II, following p. 276.

113 The piano maker Conrad Graf (1782–1851) loaned a piano to Beethoven in about
1823. It is presently in the Beethovenhaus, Bonn. It has a range of more than 6
octaves C¹–f⁴). See Frimmel, *Beethoven-Studien*, II, pp. 230–233; see also Paul
Mies, "Beethovens letzter Flügel," in *Verein Beethoven-Haus Bonn 1889–1964*
(Bonn, 1964), especially pp. 32–44; photograph, p. 33 (another photograph in
Frimmel, *Beethoven-Studien*, II, following p. 276.)

114 An uncertain tradition connects the S. A. Vogel piano with Beethoven, allegedly
as a gift from Prince Lichnowsky. For details, see Frimmel, *Beethoven-Studien*, I,
p. 22, and II, p. 233.

115 The engraving by G. Leybold is reproduced in Paul Bekker, *Beethoven*, illustrated edition (Berlin, 1911), Appendix of Illustrations, p. 139. See Plate 17.

116 In about 1800, Beethoven was presented with a quartet of instruments by Prince
Lichnowsky, consisting of a violin by Giuseppe Guarneri, another attributed to
Niccolò Amati (or Amati workshop), a viola attributed to Vicenzo Ruggieri, and
a cello attributed to Andrea Guarneri. See MacArdle, "Minor Beethoveniana
II," *Musical Quarterly*, 46 (1960), 41–42. For a photograph of the instruments,
see Joseph Schmidt-Görg and Hans Schmidt, eds., *Ludwig van Beethoven* (New
York, 1970), pp. 92–93. The instruments and the ear trumpets are in the Beet-
hovenhaus, Bonn.

117 For a photograph of the chiffonier, which is now in the Vienna City Museum,
see *Moderne Welt*, 2 no. 9 (1920), p. 7. Fräulein Leopoldine Annacker aided
A. W. Thayer during his early researches and was the dedicatee of Thayer's
Chronologisches Verzeichnis der Werke Ludwig van Beethovens (Berlin, 1865).

118 The full name of "Sali" is unknown.

119 Letter of spring 1826, in Anderson, III, pp. 1279–1280 (letter 1473). Presumably,
the journal is either the *Wiener Zeitschrift für Literatur, Theater und Mode* (the
Modenzeitung) or *Zeitung für die Elegante Welt*, both published in Vienna.

120 The paragraph derives mainly from Schindler–MacArdle, p. 386.

121 Beethoven once signed a letter to his nephew Karl, "dein Hosenknopf" (Your
trouser button). Letter of Sept. 22, 1816, in Anderson, II, p. 599 (letter 658).

122 The Berlin poet Ludwig Rellstab (1799–1860), visited Beethoven in April–May
1825 and recorded his recollections of their meetings in several writings, including

Weltgegenden: Eine Sammlung schöngeistiger Produkte der beliebtesten und berühmt-esten Dichter und Schriftsteller Deutschlands, ed. von Chlodwig [F. L. Heuke], (Cottbus, 1841), Jahrgang 1, vol. III, pp. 11–64; *Garten und Wald. Novellen und vermischte Schriften*, 4 vols. (Leipzig, 1854); and *Aus meinem Leben*, 2 vols. (Berlin, 1861), II, pp. 224–266, excerpted in Thayer–Deiters–Riemann, V, pp. 196–209 (here p. 198).

123 For Beethoven's clumsiness, see Wegeler–Ries, p. 110; Wegeler–Ries Eng. edn., p. 106.

124 The reference is to Martin Tejček's ink drawing (*c.* 1823). Historisches Museum, Vienna.

125 The quotation is from Schiller's "Ode to Joy."

126 The original is in the Beethoven–Gedenkstätte in Floridsdorf. See Dr Leopold Wech, "Ein Notizzettel von Ludwig van Beethoven in der Beethoven–Gedenk-stätte in Floridsdorf," *Wiener Beethoven–Gesellschaft Mitteilungsblatt*, no. 3 (1982), 9–11. Breuning's transcription is defective in several respects; the origi-nal reads:

† Spiegel
† ducaten
† Flanell
† Schneider
† Seife zum waschen
† Breuning
  Klavierschule

† beym Bruder	† Violin
Büsten handel [Händel?] etc.	Kasten
† Obladen	heut besorgen
† Mehl	Nachtsgeschirr

Dr. Grita Herre of the Deutsche Staatsbibliothek graciously located the auto-graph and corrected the transcription.

127 Letter of September 20, 1825, in Anderson, III, p. 1250 (letter 1432). See also Beethoven's advice to Stephan von Breuning not to use Pleyel's piano method (p. 75, above). The letters "B.r.o.t" should be "Brwt" = "Bierwirt," (ale-house proprietor).

128 Wegeler–Ries, Supplement, p. 23; Wegeler–Ries Eng. edn., pp. 158–159. Letter of late September 1826, in Anderson, III, p. 1313 (letter 1532).

129 Joseph Carl Stieler's portrait in oils of Beethoven (1819–1920). Collection Walter Hinrichsen, New York.

130 Anderson, III, pp. 1333–1334 (letter 1551).

131 Louis Letronne's drawing is best known for the engraving of it by Blasius Höfel printed by Artaria & Co. in 1814; "Chimon", and "Schiman", are Ferdinand

Schimon, painter of a portrait in oils (1818–1819); for Hornemann, see note 89, above; "Johann" Klein should be Franz Klein, the sculptor, see note 58, above; piano manufacturer and close friend of Beethoven and Schiller, Johann Andreas Streicher (1761–1833) apparently commissioned Klein's bust; he had a collection of busts of famous musicians on display in his piano salon. Also based on the life mask, Anton Dietrich exhibited several different plaster busts of Beethoven in the early 1820's. Josef Danhauser drew Beethoven's head at the post-mortem examination; he also made a death mask and a subsequent sculpture from it; "Jäger", is not identified; he may be August von Klöber, who did a charcoal and crayon portrait of Beethoven in 1818. Johann Nepomuk Schaller's posthumous bust of Beethoven (*c.* 1828) is in the Bodleian Library, Oxford. In connection with its presentation, Frau Linzbauer published a brochure entitled *Documents, Letters etc., relating to the Bust of Ludwig van Beethoven* (London, 1871). See Thayer–Deiters–Riemann, v, p. 463. Breuning omits several important Beethoven portraits: for example, those by Isidor Neugass (*c.* 1806); Willibrord Josef Mähler (1815); Johann Christoph Heckel (1815); Ferdinand Waldmüller (1823); Stefan Decker's drawing (1824); and Josef Teltscher's drawings (1827). For discussions see Frimmel, *Beethoven-Studien*, I, passim.; Frimmel, *Beethoven im zeitgenössischen Bildnis* (Vienna, 1925); Frimmel, *Handbuch*, I, pp. 41–48. For excellent modern reproductions of Beethoven portraits, see H. C. Robbins Landon, *Beethoven: A Documentary Study* (London and New York, 1970), and Schmidt-Görg and Schmidt, eds., *Ludwig van Beethoven*. William George Cusins (1833–1893)·was conductor of the Philharmonic Society from 1867 to 1883. The spurious Beethoven portrait by "Wittich" is actually a portrait of the art-dealer L. W. Wittich (see Frimmel, *Beethoven-Studien*, I, pp. 164–165). The detailed reminiscences of Beethoven by the editor and critic Johann Friedrich Rochlitz (1769–1842) are now believed to have been fabricated; the two men probably never even met. See Solomon, *Beethoven Essays*, pp. 126–138.

132 The king sent the medal to Beethoven on February 20, 1824, to express his satisfaction at receipt of a manuscript copy of the Missa solemnis, to which he had subscribed in 1823. Thayer–Forbes, pp. 828–829.

133 Breuning does not quite understand the distinction. Kalischer observes that, according to the letter from the Vienna Magistracy dated November 16, 1815, Beethoven was granted a somewhat lesser privilege – "the freedom of the city" (*Bürgerrecht*) – rather than "honorary citizen of Vienna" (*Ehrenbürger der Stadt Wien*). The award was for Beethoven's efforts in raising money for charity through the performances of his works. The Magistracy wrote that it had granted him "the freedom of the metropolis and capital city and tax-free status, bestowed as a sign of recognition of his services and the valued estimation of these good intentions." Kalischer, p. 112, note 60. See Plate 23.

134 The composer Carl Czerny (1791–1857); the piano-teacher Joseph Czerny

(1785–1831); the outstanding cellist Josef Linke (1783–1837); the violinist Carl Maria von Bocklet (1801–1881); the composers Franz Schubert (1797–1828), Joseph Weigl (1766–1846), and Josef Eybler (1765–1846); the tenor Matthäus Lutz (1807–1853).

135 The Vienna premieres of Beethoven's Ninth Symphony took place on May 7 and 23, 1824, that is, more than a year before Beethoven's reconciliation with Stephan von Breuning and two years before his offer to provide concert tickets. Young Breuning's presence at either of these concerts may be doubted.

136 Richard Wagner, "Bericht über die Aufführung der neunten Symphonie von Beethoven im Jahre 1846 in Dresden ... nebst Programm dazu," *Gesammelte Schriften und Dichtungen*, 10 vols. (Leipzig, 1871–1873, 1883), II, pp. 65–84; *Richard Wagner's Prose Works*, ed. and translated by William Ashton Ellis, 8 vols. (London, 1892–1899), VII, pp. 239–255.

137 The influential composer and musician Abbé Maximilian Stadler (1748–1833) was known to be hostile to Beethoven's music. The composer and conductor Otto Nicolai (1810–1849) featured Beethoven symphonies at the Philharmonic concerts in Vienna in the 1840s.

138 For his cooperation, Baron Josef von Stutterheim (died 1831) became the un-likely dedicatee of Beethoven's String Quartet in C-sharp minor, Op. 131 (published June 1827).

139 Breuning appears to be quoting from a police document, which does not survive. As an attempted suicide, Karl was required to receive religious instruction during his stay at the hospital. Following a hearing at the Vienna Magistracy, Beethoven resigned his guardianship in favor of Stephan von Breuning in September 1826. See Schindler–Moscheles, p. 122; Thayer–Forbes, pp. 998–1001; Thayer–Deiters–Riemann, V, pp. 362–364; Richard and Editha Sterba, *Beethoven and His Nephew*, translated by Willard Trask (New York, 1954), pp. 284–286.

140 An apocryphal anecdote by Schindler. See Schindler–MacArdle, p. 220. See Solomon, *Beethoven Essays*, p. 53.

141 Thayer–Forbes, pp. 1014–1015. Compare Schindler's malicious account in Schindler–MacArdle, pp. 317–318.

142 Such a letter does not survive.

143 Johann's wife was Therese van Beethoven, née Obermayer (1787–1828); her daughter was Amalie Waldmann (1807–1831).

144 The rondo-finale of the String Quartet, Op. 130, is its sixth, not fourth, move-ment. It was begun in Vienna, completed in Gneixendorf, and delivered to publisher Matthias Artaria on November 15, 1826.

145 The fragment (26 measures) of a String Quintet in C major (not E major), Hess 41, was published by Anton Diabelli in 1838 in arrangements for piano solo and piano four-hands (WoO 62), under the heading, "Ludwig van Beethoven's

letzter mu[?]alischer Gedanke" (Ludwig van Beethoven's last musical thought).
Nottebohm does not refer to sketches for a four-hand piano sonata. Nottebohm,
Beethoveniana, pp. 79–81.

146 The Grosse Fuge, the original finale of the String Quartet, Op. 130, was its sixth
movement. Its publisher was Matthias Artaria, not the better-known firm of
Artaria & Co.

147 Breuning adopts the carriage-story from Schindler (Schindler–Moscheles,
p. 122; Schindler–MacArdle, p. 318.) In his earliest account, a letter written to
Moscheles on February 22, 1827, Schindler told a rather different story: "On his
journey hither, he was obliged, from stress of weather, to pass the night in a
small and wretched pot-house, where he caught so bad a chill that it brought on
an immediate attack of inflammation of the lungs, and it was in this condition
that he arrived here." See Moscheles, I, p. 146. This coincides with the testimony of the attending physician. See Thayer–Forbes, p. 1016. Beethoven was
already ill, with swollen belly and limbs, when he arrived at Gneixendorf. See
Thayer–Forbes, p. 1013.

148 Dr. Andreas Wawruch (1782?–1842) became Beethoven's attending physician
after his return to Vienna from Gneixendorf.

149 For reasoned evaluations of Beethoven's medical treatment during his final
illness, see Waldemar Schweisheimer, *Beethovens Leiden: Ihr Einfluss auf sein Leben
und Schaffen* (Munich, 1922), pp. 164–203, and M. Piroth, M.D., "Beethovens
letzte Krankheit auf Grund der zeitgenössischen medizinischen Quellen," *BJ,
1959/60* (Bonn, 1962), especially pp. 22–26. Stephan Ley brings together the relevant extracts from the conversation books concerning the medical treatment. See
Ley, *Aus Beethovens Erdentagen* (Bonn, 1948), pp. 204–223.

150 If the letter existed, it has not survived.

151 This account derives entirely from Schindler (see Schindler–Moscheles, p. 123,
Schindler–MacArdle, p. 318). MacArdle comments: "The actual course of
events during Beethoven's 1st week in Vienna ... is completely different from
that stated by Schindler ... It is difficult to see how Schindler can be absolved of
the charge of having prepared a cruel fabrication, known by him to be false from
beginning to end, for the purpose of vilifying the nephew ..." Schindler–
MacArdle, p. 358, note 252. In actuality it was Holz who summoned Dr.
Wawruch.

152 English translation in Sonneck, pp. 221–226.

153 Although Beethoven was not an alcoholic, his inclination for alcoholic beverages
is well documented and is presumed to have played some part in the etiology of
his cirrhosis of the liver. See references in note 149 above. Schindler continued
his attack on Wawruch's report in Schindler–MacArdle, pp. 457–459.

154 Breuning noted that "the box and the writing desk are in my possession." Kalischer, p. 132, note 65a.

155 See note 138 above.

156 Between December 20, 1826 and February 27, 1827, Johann Seibert, Chief Surgeon at the Vienna General Hospital, performed four operations on Beethoven to relieve his dropsy.

157 Anton Braunhofer (1773 or *c.* 1781–1846), one of Vienna's leading physicians, to whom Beethoven dedicated his "Abendlied unterm gestirnten Himmel," WoO 150 (1820), attended the composer between 1820 and 1826. He treated him for rheumatism and gout in February–March 1826, coming readily in response to Beethoven's letter to him of February 1826 (Anderson, III, p. 1278 [letter 1471]). Jakob Staudenheim (1764–1830) had been Beethoven's physician for a decade, beginning in 1812. Staudenheim did consult with Dr. Wawruch in December 1826 and agreed with his course of treatment; and he probably participated in a further consultation on January 11, 1827. Breuning's speculation that the doctors feared inadequate fees is unfair and unsupported. Braunhofer would not accept payment from Beethoven in early 1826; he clearly he hoped for another dedication. See Köhler–Herre–Beck, IX, pp. 147–148. One scholar suggests that Braunhofer "didn't want to be the doctor who killed Beethoven by doctoring." Walter Nohl, "Beethoven und sein Arzt Anton Braunhofer," *Die Musik*, 30 (1938), 823–828 (here p. 828).

158 Against this view, one must note Dr. Wawruch's calmly professional efforts to treat Beethoven and to make him comfortable during his decline; he visited him at least daily and sometimes as often as three times per day. For a cogent defense of Wawruch against Schindler, see Ley, *Wahrheit, Zweifel und Irrtum in der Kunde von Beethovens Leben* (Wiesbaden, 1955), pp. 38–39.

159 Dr. Giovanni (Johann) Malfatti (1775–1859), with whose family Beethoven was closely acquainted in 1809–1810, and who had earlier been one of Beethoven's physicians. He was brought in as a consulting physician in January 1827.

160 The passage in quotation marks may be a paraphrase of Schindler. See Schindler–MacArdle, pp. 320, 458.

161 The Samuel Arnold edition of the works of Handel in 40 volumes (published 1787–1797) was a gift to Beethoven from the London harp-manufacturer Johann Andreas Stumpff (1769–1846); the set arrived in Vienna in December 1826 and was acknowledged in a letter to Stumpff dated February 8, 1827. See receipt of December 14, 1826, Anderson, III, p. 1433 (Appendix G, 19) and Anderson, III, p. 1332 (letter 1550).

162 In interviews during his last decade with such Londoners as Stumpff, Cipriani Potter, and J. R. Schulz, Beethoven repeatedly referred to Handel as "the greatest composer who ever lived." See Thayer–Deiters–Riemann, IV, pp. 57 and 457, and V, p. 126. In 1796, he composed Variations for Piano and Violin on a theme from *Judas Maccabeus*, WoO 45, but Handelian influences appear particularly in such late works as the Missa solemnis, Op. 123, the 33 Vari-

ations on a Theme by Diabelli, Op. 120, and the Overture, *Die Weihe des Hauses*,
Op. 124.

163 The conversation book entry has not been located. Premieres by Schuppanzigh
of the Quartet in E-flat major, Op. 127 (March 6, 1825), and of the Quartet in
B-flat major, Op. 130 (March 21, 1826) had mixed receptions. But during the
period Breuning refers to there was only a successful private performance of the
new finale for the Quartet in B-flat, Op. 130, in December 1826.

164 Breuning's footnote is entirely derived from Schindler (Schindler–MacArdle,
pp. 444–445). It is untrue that all of Beethoven's works apart from the symphonies and quartets had disappeared from the repertory. Beethoven's copy of
Goethe's *West-östlicher Divan* (Vienna and Stuttgart, 1820) is in DSB, Berlin,
autograph 40,1; the underscored passage, from the introduction to Chapter 36, is
reprinted in Nohl, *Beethovens Brevier*, p. 86. The passage was not copied into
Beethoven's Tagebuch.

165 Shortly before his death, in gratitude for the gift of £100 from the Philharmonic
Society, which was led to believe him to be penniless, Beethoven offered to
compose for the Philharmonic Society " a new symphony, sketches for which are
already in my desk, or a new overture, or something else which the society might
like to have." Letter to Ignaz Moscheles of March 18, 1827, Anderson, III,
p. 1544 (letter 1566). For the details and controversy surrounding Beethoven's
solicitation of the gift, see Moscheles, I, pp. 144–188. For the surviving sketches
for the first movement of a tenth symphony see Cooper, "Newly Identified
Sketches for Beethoven's Tenth Symphony," pp. 9–18; also Robert S. Winter,
"Of Realizations, Completions, Restorations and Reconstructions: From Bach's
The Art of Fugue to Beethoven's Tenth Symphony," *Journal of the Royal Musical
Association*, 116 (1991), 96–125. See note 93 above.

166 One may reasonably question whether the entire preceding discussion of musical
matters actually took place, for its components – Beethoven's search for a suitable opera subject, his disavowal of "disreputable" librettos, the alleged failure
of *Fidelio*, and future plans, etc. – all appear to derive from published sources,
including Schindler, Rochlitz, and Ludwig Rellstab. Breuning's exaggeration of
the neglect of Beethoven's music, here and elsewhere, is taken from Rochlitz's
fabricated account (see Thayer–Forbes, p. 801). Beethoven had mixed feelings
about Mozart's librettos: Seyfried, an excellent witness, quotes him as referring
to *Don Giovanni* as a "scandalous subject" (Sonneck, p. 44), but Beethoven once
wrote, "The good reception of Mozart's Don Juan gives me as much pleasure as
if it were my own work." Letter of August 23, 1811, to Breitkopf & Härtel,
Anderson, I, p. 334 (letter 323). Breuning's account of Beethoven's distaste for
Mozart's librettos derives from Rellstab's questionable report (Wegeler–Ries,
Supplement, p. 15–16; Wegeler Ries Eng. edn., p. 153; see Thayer–Forbes,
p. 947). Antonio Diabelli (1781–1858) and Tobias Haslinger (1787–1842)

were important Viennese publishers; Beethoven was much attached to Haslinger.

167 The description is of a Beethoven sketchbook.

168 The scholar and collector Aloys Fuchs (1799–1853) owned numerous Beethoven memorabilia and manuscripts, including the Grasnick 2 and Wittgenstein sketchbooks. It was the latter which Fuchs gave to Felix Mendelssohn in 1830. See Richard Schaal, *Quellen und Forschungen zur Wiener Musiksammlung von Aloys Fuchs* (Vienna, 1966); Douglas Johnson, Alan Tyson, and Robert Winter, *The Beethoven Sketchbooks*, ed. Douglas Johnson (Berkeley and Los Angeles, 1985), pp. 16–17 and passim.

169 A copy of the lithograph of Haydn's birthplace in Rohrau sold at Diabelli & Co. is in the Bildarchiv of the Österreichische Nationalbibliothek (see Plate 28). Rohrau is in Lower Austria, not Moravia, and Haydn's family was well-off, not "poverty-stricken," as Breuning writes.

170 "Thon" = old spelling for "clay."

171 Heribert Rau (see note 8 above) is mistakenly called "Rauch" by Breuning; Bohemian composer Jan Emanuel Doležálek (1780–1858); the violinist Franz Clement (see note 43 above).

172 The famous soprano Nanette Schechner (1806–1860) visited Beethoven in mid-February 1827 together with her fiancé, tenor Ludwig Cramolini (died 1884). Johann Nepomuk Hummel and his wife Elisabeth Röckel (see note 95 above), along with his young student, the composer-conductor Ferdinand Hiller (1811–1885) visited on March 8, 13, and 23.

173 For Hiller's affecting accounts, see Thayer–Forbes, pp. 1045–1047; Sonneck, pp. 214–219.

174 Marie Egloff (see note 103 above); "Baron Gleichenberg" is Beethoven's intimate friend Baron Ignaz von Gleichenstein (1778–1828), who visited the deathbed several times, once with his wife and son. Thayer–Forbes, p. 1037.

175 Ignaz Moscheles, letter to Beethoven of March 1, 1827. See Schindler–Moscheles, p. 127; Schindler–MacArdle, p. 323. See note 165 above.

176 For the testimony of Wawruch, Schindler, and Anselm Hüttenbrenner concerning Beethoven's acceptance of the last rites, see Ley, *Wahrheit, Zweifel und Irrtum*, pp. 39–40.

177 Schindler–MacArdle, p. 324; see Schindler–MacArdle, p. 360, note 266 for MacArdle's discussion of this disputed topic; see also Thayer–Forbes, p. 1048, note 53. For the various "last words" attributed to Beethoven, see Frimmel, *Handbuch*, I, pp. 343–344; see also Kalischer, p. 155, note 69.

178 See Solomon, "The Quest for Faith," in *Beethoven Essays*, pp. 216–229.

179 Stephan von Breuning had been appointed Karl's guardian in September 1826. Beethoven's attorney was Johann Baptist Bach (1779–1847), professor of law at Vienna University. One of the documents given to Beethoven for his signature

was the codicil to his will, dated March 23, 1827: "My nephew Karl shall be my sole legatee, but the capital of my estate shall fall to his natural or testamentary heirs." Anderson, III, p. 1346 (letter 1568). If Gerhard von Breuning is correct that Beethoven signed the testamentary letter to Bach – in addition to the codicil – just before his death, the letter may have been deliberately backdated to January 3, 1827.

180 Anderson, III, p. 1329 (letter 1547).

181 For a facsimile of the codicil, see Ley, *Beethovens Leben in authentischen Bildern und Texten* (Berlin, 1925), p. 140. For a discussion of Beethoven's last writings and signatures, see Max Unger, "Beethovens letzte Briefe und Unterschriften," *Die Musik*, 34 (1942), 153–158.

182 In his earliest account, Hüttenbrenner identified Frau van Beethoven as Johanna van Beethoven, nephew Karl's mother, rather than Johann's wife, Therese van Beethoven. See H. E. Krehbiel, *Music and Manners in the Classical Period* (New York, 1898), p. 204. It has been speculated that Hüttenbrenner mistook for one of Beethoven's sisters-in-law the housekeeper Sali. See Thayer–Forbes, p. 1051. Josef Teltscher made three drawings picturing Beethoven on his death-bed (see Bekker, *Beethoven*, Appendix of Illustrations, pp. 143–145.) See Plate 29.

183 Probably this is "Beethoven auf dem Totenbett" (no painter designated) once in the Musikhistorischen Museum des Herrn F. N. Manskopf, Frankfurt, and reproduced in Fritz Volbach, *Beethoven* (Mainz, 1905, reprinted 1929), p. 106 (fig. 59). The original has disappeared. See Plate 30.

184 In addition to taking a death mask, the artist Josef Danhauser (1805–1845) made a drawing of the dead Beethoven on March 28, 1827, which was widely distributed as a lithograph.

185 Following Schindler's erroneous identification (Schindler–MacArdle, pp. 104–105), Breuning believed that Beethoven's letter to the "Immortal Beloved," dated July 6–7, 1812 (Anderson, I, pp. 373–376 [letter 373]), was addressed to Countess Guicciardi (1784–1856). Modern scholarship identifies the addressee as most probably Antonie Brentano (see note 90 above). A facsimile and transcription of the letter is in Sieghard Brandenburg, *Beethoven: Der Brief an die Unsterbliche Geliebte* (Bonn, 1986). Accounts vary as to the remaining contents of the drawer and whether it was in a desk, a strongbox, or a cupboard. See Thayer–Deiters–Riemann, V, p. 493 and note 1; Thayer–Krehbiel, III, pp. 309–310. In a letter to Kalischer, Breuning wrote that these issues cannot be precisely solved and indicated that he had no real knowledge of the matter: "This much is clear: the letter and such things were either in some side drawer or some so-called secret compartment, along with small miniature portraits ... " Letter of November 6, 1891, see Ley, *Beethoven als Freund*, p. 255.

186 For the Autopsy Report by the pathologist Dr. Johann Wagner, see Thayer–Forbes, pp. 1059–1060.

187 The authenticity of the so-called "Hyrtl-skull," which was exhumed in 1801 and is now in the Mozart Museum in Salzburg, is still the subject of controversy. See Gustav Gugitz, "Mozart's Schädel und Dr. Gall," *Zeitschrift für Musikwissenschaft* 16 (1934), 32–39, reprinted in Gugitz, *Mozartiana* (Vienna, 1964), pp. 74–84; Peter J. Davies, *Mozart in Person: His Character and Health* (New York, Westport, and London, 1989), pp. 171–4.

188 The famous impresario Domenico Barbaia (?1778–1841) managed the Kärntnertortheater and the Theater an der Wien from 1821 to 1828.

189 Eybler (see note 134 above); Hummel (see note 95 above); Ignaz von Seyfried (1776–1841); Kreutzer (see note 97 above); Weigl (see note 134 above); Adalbert Gyrowetz (1763–1850); Wilhelm Würfl (1791–1852); and Johann Gänsbacher (1778–1844).

190 Schindler's apocryphal story about the decoration or the ducats relates to the Missa solemnis, not the Ninth Symphony. Schindler–MacArdle, p. 241. For the gift of the ring in exchange for the dedication of the Symphony, see Solomon, *Beethoven*, pp. 288–289. For the letter to Wegeler, which is actually dated December 7 (not October 7), 1826, see Anderson, III, p. 1322 (letter 1542). See note 3 above.

191 The outstanding court actor Heinrich Anschütz (1785–1865) met Beethoven in 1822.

192 We have used the translation by O. G. Sonneck, in Sonneck, pp. 229–231, reprinted in Thayer–Forbes, pp. 1057–1058. Breuning's text varies in several details from Grillparzer's published text of the oration; translations of the variants follow, omitting those which do not affect the meaning in translation.

    1. Breuning: "pious" for "humble."

    2. Breuning: "Song's Muse" for "Muse of song."

    3. Added, in Breuning: "rather he arises and thrusts outward."

    4. Breuning: "tenderest" for "finest."

    5. Breuning: "foothold" for "weapon."

    6. Breuning: "because they would not ascend to him and he could not descend to them," for "after he had given them his all and received nothing in return."

    7. Added, in Breuning: "this funeral procession."

    8. From here to the end, Breuning: "For it is not a depressing but rather an uplifting feeling to stand at the coffin of the man of whom one may say, as of no-one else: he achieved greatness and was deserving of no reproach. Carry your mourning with you, but with resolution. Take with you a flower from his grave – in memory of him and his works. And should you ever in times to come feel the overpowering might of his creations like an onrushing storm, then recall the memory of today, the memory of him, who achieved such greatness and upon whom fell no reproach."

193 The poet and censor Johann Gabriel Seidl (1804–1875) was a member of the Schubert circle. Schubert set several of his poems.

194 The prolific author Ignaz Franz Castelli (1781–1862) was an acquaintance of Beethoven's from about 1811 onwards. We have used the translation by Arthur Duke Coleridge, from Moscheles, I, pp. 166–167. Baron Franz von Schlechta (1796–1875).

195 Breuning retells this melodramatic story, which is of doubtful provenance, from Kreissle von Hellborn, *The Life of Schubert*, 2 vols. (London, 1869), I, pp. 268–269. An entry in Fritz von Hartmann's diary describing Schubert's actions on the night in question appears to render the anecdote moot. See Otto Erich Deutsch, *Schubert: A Documentary Biography* (London, 1946), p. 623.

196 According to Schindler, writing in 1831. See Schindler, "On Schubert's Fantasia for Four Hands, Op. 103," reprinted in Deutsch, *Schubert: Memoirs by His Friends* (London, 1958), p. 307. Schindler adds: "Should anyone doubt the truth of this fact, I am prepared to place before him the written conversation with Beethoven concerning it, which I still preserve ... " (p. 308). The alleged conversation-book evidence does not exist. More reliably, Josef Hüttenbrenner's letter of August 14, 1822 to the publisher C. F. Peters quotes Beethoven as saying, "This one will surpass me." Deutsch, *Schubert: A Documentary Biography*, p. 232.

197 The renowned Italian bass, Luigi Lablache (1794–1858), was a star of Barbaia's company.

198 The tomb of Archduchess Maria Christina, sculpted in marble 1798–1805 by the renowned Italian sculptor, Antonio Canova (1757–1822).

199 For a photograph of the black box, Ley, *Beethoven als Freund*, p. 187. See Plate 15.

200 For a photograph of the serving ladle, Ley, *Beethoven als Freund*, p. 187. See Plate 15.

201 One of the two miniature portraits on ivory is of Countess Guicciardi (see note 185 above), the wife of Count Robert Gallenberg (1783–1839); the other, though mistakenly assumed to be of Countess Marie Erdödy (1779–1837), is almost certainly of Antonie Brentano (see notes 90 and 185 above). For a photograph of the compass, Ley, *Beethoven als Freund*, p. 187.

202 For a photograph of Beethoven's gravestone at Währing Cemetery, Ley, *Beethovens Leben in authentischen Bildern*, p. 149. See also Plate 31.

203 A portrait in oils by Leopold Gross. Historisches Museum, Vienna.

204 Johanna van Beethoven, née Reiss (*c.* 1786–1868).

205 For their names and dates, see Schmidt-Görg, *Beethoven: Die Geschichte seiner Familie* (Bonn and Munich, 1964), pp. 119–124.

206 See note 9 above.

207 See note 92 above.

208 The following discussion of Beethoven's and Schubert's skulls is expanded in

Breuning's "Die Schädel Beethoven's and Schubert's," *Neue Freie Presse*, 17 Sept. 1886, reprinted in Kalischer, pp. 209–221.

209 Breuning exaggerates (especially about *Fidelio*: see note 54 above) but it is true that Beethoven's last works were neglected for more than a decade in Vienna after his death.

210 Nicolai (see note 137 above); the violin virtuoso Josef Hellmesberger (1828–1893); Clara Schumann (1819–1896); the conductor and composer Johann Herbeck (1831–1877); the conductor Felix Otto Dessoff (1835–1892).

211 The first movement of a Violin Concerto in C major (Fragment), WoO 5, begun about 1790–1792 in Bonn, was completed by Hellmesberger and published in 1879 with a dedication to Gerhard von Breuning.

INDEX

Figures in italics refer to captions

780.924
B.4157BR

92615

LINCOLN CHRISTIAN COLLEGE AND SEMINARY

3 4711 00093 1073